FLIRTING WITH THE WORLD

Other books by John White:

The Cost of Commitment
Daring to Draw Near: People in Prayer
Eros Defiled: The Christian and Sexual Sin
The Fight
The Golden Cow
The Iron Sceptre
Parents in Pain
The Tower of Geburah

JOHN WHITE

FLIRTING WITH THE WORLD

A CHALLENGE TO LOYALTY

HODDER AND STOUGHTON
LONDON SYDNEY AUCKLAND TORONTO

STL BOOKS, BROMLEY

STL Books are published by Send The Light (Operation Mobilisation),
P.O. Box 48, Bromley, Kent.

British Library Cataloguing in Publication Data

White, John, *1924 – Mar. 5 –*
  Flirting with the world.
  1. Church and the world.
  I. Title
  261   BR115.W6

Hodder & Stoughton ISBN 0 340 32474 0
STL ISBN 0 903843 63 3

Hodder and Stoughton Editorial Office: 47 Bedford Square, London WC1B 3DP

to Mrs. Mildred Penner
whose unflagging and careful hours of
work have made the difference
in book after book

CONTENTS

FOREWORD   9

PROLOGUE   15

1 THE UNUSUAL ARRANGEMENT   17
2 CULTURE AND WORLDLINESS   27
3 ON STRAINING AT GNATS   39
4 SLAVERY—MODERN STYLE   53
5 TUNED IN AND TURNED ON   63
6 THE WORLD AND SEXUAL MORALITY   71
7 THE WORLD AND THE HOMOSEXUAL   83
8 DOING AS THE ROMANS DO   95
9 PSYCHOLOGY AS RELIGION   113
10 THE TRUMPET WITH THE UNCERTAIN SOUND   127
11 HOW CHRISTIANS CAN CHANGE & GROW   135
12 TO WHOM DO WE GIVE OUR LOYALTY?   147

EPILOGUE   153

FOREWORD

Worldliness is the greatest threat to the church today. In other ages the church has suffered from dead orthodoxy, live heresy, flight from the world, and other maladies. But the painful truth today is that the church is guilty of massive accommodation to the world. It is this worldliness which John White here unmasks with skill, force, and compassion.

When I was a boy, people talked about worldliness. We knew what it was. Within our little evangelical counter-culture worldliness became, in fact, a battle cry. Cracks developed in our fellowships over different perceptions of the "worldliness" creeping into our churches. We knew that worldliness was more a problem in some areas than others: In Michigan, where I grew up, people in the rural north thought those of us in the more urban and urbane south were becoming hopelessly worldly. Maybe they were right, but in the wrong way.

We knew what worldliness *was,* back then in the fifties. Worldliness meant lipstick and make-up, short skirts and bobbed hair, wedding rings and jewelry, movies and church kitchens. Strangely, many of the issues had to do with how women dressed. Now these things are no longer issues, but the question of who won and who lost is not neatly clear.

The battle over worldliness in our Free Methodist sub-culture was a product of the times. It was geared to the emerging postwar economic boom and the rise of the suburban protestant middle class which produced so many of today's white church leaders. Those who fought the liberalizing trends of education, affluence, mobility, and urbanization may have pitched the battle in the wrong places, but we can't fault their instincts. They knew something vital was at stake: *the maintenance of a distinct identity.* Once we gave in to the world's pressures, and "let the world into the church," what would be left?

We gave in, of course, and many of our leaders hailed this as progress. Now the enemy was not "worldliness" but "legalism," and we praised the move from narrow rules to "personal convictions."

Much of this was, indeed, progress. There were more important things to fight over than lipstick and wedding rings (or similar issues in other contexts). The problem was that we didn't know how to sort out the real issues of worldliness from the pseudo-issues. The problem wasn't that the emerging suburban evangelical middle class shed certain taboos of the past; the problem was that they failed to build the kind of churches where new issues of worldliness could be discerned and where authentic Christian community could be experienced.

In giving in to middle-class affluence, many Christians also gave in to the selfism and individualism of the fifties and sixties. Here is the crux: Christians were set loose to pursue money, power, prestige, and status, *with no one to call them to account.* Individualism has, of course, a long history in Western culture; it is not a new thing. But in recent decades it has become the door through which a new kind of worldliness has overtaken the church with a vengeance.

For these reasons, we need a new sorting out of the real issues of worldliness today. This is what John White does with considerable success. He shows what real worldliness is and is not. He is forthright in maintaining biblical standards of sexuality and personal morality. But he also points to the equally important but often more subtle issues of worldliness tied up with the quest for affluence, the worship of success, the conceit of patriotism, and the psychology of selfism. Here he shows, convincingly, how thoroughly even the most conservative and fundamentalist churches have capitulated to worldliness.

I believe the author is on target when he brings all these issues down to two fundamental points: Proper inductive study and teaching of the Bible, and the shape of the church. As Dr. White shows, the Bible—not certain key doctrines or pet doctrinal quirks, but *the Bible* in its broad sweep—is strangely silent in too many of our churches. We teach as Scripture the traditions of men and ignore or distort plain Scriptures that speak of the kind of life we are to live in the world. We have twisted Paul's words, "Live a life worthy of the calling you have received" (Eph. 4:1 NIV) to mean "Live a life of success, prosperity, and achievement, and God will be pleased." Such Christianity certainly has no place for oddballs like Abraham, Moses, Jeremiah, or Amos—to say nothing of the one who "did not come to be served, but to serve, and to give his life as a ransom for many" (Matt. 20:28 NIV).

Most of all, the issue of worldliness raises the question of our corporate life together: what it means to be the church. Like Philipp Spener in seventeenth-century Germany, John Wesley in eighteenth-century England, and many others before and since, Dr. White calls Christians back to an experience of the church and to the formation of small cells where Christian life together can be discovered and the true dimensions of discipleship explored earnestly and in depth. Here is the lesson the church constantly forgets and has to relearn: To be a Christian means to be part of a people. To be a faithful believer means to be part of a faithful believing community. To be joined to the Head means to be joined to the Body. And to resist worldliness requires embracing covenant community. In our day, especially, the only hope for authentic Christianity is a community of believers so radically committed to Jesus and to each other that it is willing to be countercultural at the point of the world's idolatries and adulteries.

John White's is one of a growing chorus of voices calling for a new awareness of worldliness and a new commitment to the biblical gospel. We will not all see the issues in precisely the same way, and so we need to listen to each other. But together, with God's guidance, we can identify the true enemy, learn to be the church, and find our base in Jesus Christ—and thus be the salt and light of God's Kingdom in a crooked and perverse generation.

Howard A. Snyder
Chicago, Illinois

PROLOGUE

Cohabitation they call it. Living together. No, they're not married. As a matter of fact she is engaged to Someone Else—and is rather smugly vain about the fact.

Hard to understand, isn't it? You'd think she'd be more discreet. I mean it *looks bad*. I don't know what she sees in him (in her boyfriend, Mundo—not her fiancé) and I'm certain he doesn't respect her. He merely tolerates and uses her. I think she's too uncertain of herself and tries too hard to please to win any real admiration from him. Strange what some girls will do to hold on to a man!

They say her fiancé is not only hurt but enraged. He writes letters to her—pleading and furious letters—

though it seems he still plans to go ahead with the wedding. I wouldn't have blamed him if he'd dropped her. The whole affair is so puzzling; you'd think that she'd be scared to death of him. I mean his anger is *something else*. I'd be shaking in my boots if I'd received the kind of letters he sends her. Says he's going to "purify" her, and buy her a white wedding gown. Certainly an unusual relationship, don't you think? And she —so blithely carrying on with the boyfriend on the side.

Cohabitation. Living together. Do they sleep together? Well, one can only suppose so. Curiously, her fiancé seems to have no objection to their occupying the same living quarters. He seems to feel it's all right for them to share the apartment but not the bedroom. Certainly an unusual situation—*in* the place but not *of* it. Well, she's certainly in, and every indication points to her being rather more *of* than she has any right to be.

You say I'm gossiping? That I should mind my own business? That I'm in no position to point a finger? Well, *someone* has to speak out. You may be right in calling me flippant, or a gossip, or presumptuous. I know, I know, you don't have to tell me. She's to become a royal princess and who am I—blah, blah, blah. But surely you see my point. I don't intend to pontificate—I'm just urging her to read those letters again. *His letters*. They're what matter. And getting her act cleaned up. And learning what true love and loyalty are all about.

1
THE UNUSUAL ARRANGEMENT

*I do not pray that thou
shouldst take them out of the world,
but that thou shouldst keep
them from the Evil One. They are not
of the world . . (John 17:15-18).*

I N, BUT NOT OF. There, so to speak, but not belonging.
It would make matters so much simpler if some mutual
understanding existed about the delicate arrangement,
some understanding by church and world alike of the
necessity of mutual toleration, of mutual trust, of living
and letting live.

The historical perspective
But all the evidence, biblical and postbiblical, points in
the opposite direction. For two thousand years, everything conceivable from murderous hostility on the
world's part to escape or compromise or retaliation on
the part of the church make fascinating and frightening

reading. From time to time the church has dodged the issue by aiming at being neither *of* nor *in*. Hermits, ascetics and some (but not all) monastic orders have pursued purity and sanctity by withdrawing from the abrasions and seductions of the world. Their seclusion reduced the pressures and taught them important lessons about community living and community worship. But, in spite of every effort, monastic enclaves have commonly failed to keep the world out. Worldly pollution came in not only with ransacking, rampaging heathen hordes but with every raw novice, so that carnal weeds sprouted among gardens devoted to holiness and impure thoughts flowered in the most strictly sanctified souls. It was possible for monastics to get out of the world, but far more difficult to get the world out of the monastics. Viewed in the light of being "in but not of," monasticism was not a thorough-going success.

But there were exceptions, attempts to create communities within the larger, secular community. Monks and nuns of various orders sought to be lumps of heavenly leaven. They did so by leading disciplined lives of worship combined with service to the community at large. They taught such things as music, calligraphy, farming methods, set up hostels and soup kitchens, cared for the dying, stored and shared knowledge, became living examples of charity and chastity. They even ventured forth in holy armies to preach the good news, to negotiate peace between warring tribes and to baptize heathen chieftains and their villagers. Much of the story of the declining power of the druids, in third- and fourth-century Britain, seems to have stemmed from the work of monastics like Columba of Iona, who sacrificed his royal prerogatives to devote his life to preaching the gospel of Christ as he understood it.

Columba, or Columcille as he was more commonly called, hazarded his life for the principles he stood for and taught. His song of faith pays tribute to his spirit.

God's elect are safe
Even on the battlefront.
No man can kill me before my day
Even in close combat;
No one can save me
When the hour of death comes.
No magic can tell my fate,
No bird on twig on crooked oak.
The voice of birds I do not idolize,
Nor luck, nor love of son or wife.
My druid is Christ, the son of God.

(Reginald B. Hale, *The Magnificent Gale* [World Media, 1976] p. 62.)

Ignorant and prejudiced as we evangelicals are about the long history of monasticism, we either ignore or else too quickly condemn the movement. In spite of human sin and frailty, possessing only fragments of the Gospels (carefully copied by hand, on vellum), the monastics conserved and channeled the light of Scripture. The Celtic monastic tradition, in particular, preserved the knowledge of Christ and paved the way for later movements of the Holy Spirit in Britain. (See John T. McNeill, *A History of the Cure of Souls* [New York: Harper & Row, 1977].)

Among the benefits for those who became a part of monastic communities were the close fellowship with those of like mind, the disciplines of silence and worship, the opportunity to deal with and confess sin and to seek wise counsel, and the exposure to the Scriptures which were not available to the general populace. Though many of these restrictions encouraged personal purity and spirituality, they were undoubtedly galling and painful. The loss of personal freedom and choice would have been among the most difficult trials to bear.

But today few of us are monastics. We deny ourselves both the benefits and the drawbacks of such communities of light. And so we must ask ourselves, in what sense are we called to be *not of the world*?

Not of the world

"All men shall hate you because of me," Jesus warned his followers (Matt. 10:22 NIV). The negative *not of,* then, means to be identified with Christ, to be *of Jesus,* and therefore detested by those who detest all that he stands for.

"Blessed are you when people insult you, persecute you and falsely say all kinds of evil against you because of me" (Matt. 5:11 NIV). *Not of* means that we will inevitably arouse slander and hostility, not because we are socially incompetent, conceited, priggish, or pharisaical (none of which we should be, but all of which we sometimes are) but because we obey and trust solely in our Lord. The question arises, does our present popularity, our common freedom from slander and hostility, imply that we are *not* obeying and following Christ, or that, like Peter, we follow him from afar?

And was the hostility predicted by Jesus to be universal? If we are to God "the aroma of Christ" as Paul puts it, we will inevitably be a stench in the nostrils of some people but just as surely the sweet fragrance of life and hope to others (2 Cor. 2:14-16). As they observe us, some will be disgusted and vindictive. Others will be moved and drawn irresistibly by whatever it is in our lives that speaks of Christ.

Being *not of*, then, means neither that we avoid non-Christian people and institutions, nor that we need anticipate universal rejection. Our failure commonly arises from our ability to exude only odors that are neither a stench nor a perfume. We are too bland, too insipid. We merge into the landscape too easily. We take on a camouflage of local coloring. Or if we do try to witness, it is a self-conscious posture, a condescension. We shout, we entertain, we put on amateurish acts and expect the unbelievers to take it or leave it, hoping they will realize the heady privilege of becoming one of us.

The threat
There is something about a genuine difference (and I use the word genuine to distinguish the real from the postured) which threatens others. White crows are killed off by black crows. Bees that buzz into the wrong hive are quickly stung to death. Minorities are generally treated with paranoia and suspicion. Even if the difference has nothing to do with the things of God, any tendency towards uniqueness will always be regarded with suspicion by those from whom we differ.

But there is something even more deadly about the difference our Lord demands. Because we are light we oppose the lord of darkness. Light penetrates. In any ultimate sense it always has and always will overcome the darkness. We may conceal our light, but we can do nothing to diminish its power. The tiniest flaring match invades the shadows and shines to the depths of the darkest cavern. Men love darkness because, being servants of the lord of darkness, they dread the terror of exposure almost as much as does their leader himself.

The Christians' presence also (as all the commentators testify) exerts a *preserving* effect, preventing the tendency of human societies to degenerate into chaos, confusion, and perversion. Our light is also salt and the fact that we "taste" so salty is a guarantee of our preservative qualities. We must never isolate ourselves within plastic envelopes or glass containers. As Becky Pippert puts it, we must be shaken "out of the salt-shaker into the world."

But we will never belong. We are pilgrims and strangers whose citizenship is somewhere else. Earthly governments will, in general, barely tolerate us (present conditions in the West being exceptional and temporary). Our earthly citizenship will ultimately clash with our heavenly. Historically, Christian believers are enemy agents who (under many tyrannical regimes) have found their greatest victories in the hours of their deaths.

But I pause as I write. *Am I* different? Too often, I take on local color for self-protection, trading quips for quips, blending far too easily with my surroundings. How should I be different from the world? (And what is *the world?*) Do I carry the aroma of Christ? What is the aroma of Christ? Am I really unworldly? Again, what exactly is *the world?* A crowd of rebels and sinners? (And then I remember how Jesus mingled with harlots, traitors, and those Roman collaborators despised by the zealots.)

The world—a portrait
"Do not love the world, or the things in the world. . . . For

22

all that is in the world, the lust of the flesh and the lust of the eyes and the pride of life, is not of the Father but is of the world" (1 John 2:15-16 RSV).

I used to read twice daily those collections of Scripture verses that constitute a devotional classic called *Daily Light*. In *Daily Light* there are many fascinating juxtapositions of Scripture verses. One such reading concerns Satan's first temptation to Eve. Passages from Old and New Testaments are joined to produce this: "And when the woman saw that the tree was good for food (*the lust of the flesh*) pleasant to the eyes (*the lust of the eyes*) and to be desired to make one wise (*the pride of life*) she took of the fruit thereof. . . ." *Daily Light* links the phrases with the temptations of Jesus:

"And the devil said unto him, 'If you are the Son of God, command this stone to become bread' " (Luke 4:3 RSV). (*The lust of the flesh*)

"And the devil took him up, and showed him all the kingdoms of the world in a moment of time" (Luke 4:5 RSV). (*The lust of the eyes and the pride of life*)

Though the implied exegesis may be questioned, it will serve as a rough start. Perhaps worldliness, or the spirit of the age, as we should more accurately define it, is closely associated with lusts—legitimate desires pursued or exalted to the point of idolatry.

Set in a modern context, the lusts of the flesh would include sex, food, warmth, sleep, luxury, sensuality, soft sheets, thick carpeting, good wines, and fine dining. These may all be blessings from God, but when ardently sought for themselves, rather than as gifts to be received with thankfulness, they reduce us to the status of slaves.

Current evangelical literature promises, for example, the ultimate in Christian copulation (Christianity gives you a better climax). The plethora of Christian cookbooks gives the seal of approval to gourmet food and drink, implying that we deserve them. They are our right. And the list lengthens.

There are also the lusts of the eye, the nice things of "the good life." Cars, gardens, paintings, clothes (color-coordinated and chic), jewelry, vacation cottages, exotic settings for our Christian conferences and conventions. Nothing wrong with them. The gifts of a generous God. But once again, their desirability and their importance have been blown out of proportion. They have become the necessities. We collect them ardently, and we worship what we collect. In the spirit of the age we lust for things.

And "the pride of life"? This, most of all, typifies the spirit of the age, the age that plunged into darkness with humanity's fall and will terminate under the edict of divine judgment on all our race, but is ruled by proud Lucifer until that judgment.

Those readings in *Daily Light* scratch where the itch is. We have fashioned "Christianized" sensual delights into idols to be worshiped (or idols that humiliate and enslave us), we have forged our possessions into chains that bind us to a deteriorating economy, and we have exalted pride, the pride of life, into a god who compels us to humiliate our fellow human beings by our arrogance and selfishness. All the lusts in the end become one lust—heightened sensual enjoyments, superior life styles, what we crave for ourselves becomes so compelling that we ignore God and human beings and thus are alienated from them.

To be *in, but not of* means to be delivered from the spirit of the age and to walk in liberty as sons and daughters of God. Paul describes our context in Philippians 2:15 as being "in the midst of a crooked and perverse generation among whom we are to shine as lights" in the darkness of death. Such scriptural words carry weight and conviction, but we have heard them often enough to be dulled to their sting. What do they *mean*?

Let us be more specific. We have said that to be *not of* means to be different, and this difference is critical. Perhaps we have begun to sense in what general areas we should be different, but as we look at Christian behavior in a more detailed way we may discover a multitude of perplexities and hazards.

And first, we must beware of the danger of straining at gnats (Matt. 23:24).

Questions for Study and Discussion

1. How has the church historically avoided the problem of being *in,* but not *of,* the world?

2. What is the basic reason for the world's hostility to Christians? How do most Christians respond to this hostility, both positively and negatively?

3. Describe the effects of the Christian community on the world in both positive and negative terms.

4. How do you, as a Christian, see yourself as different from your non-Christian friends?

5. Describe worldliness in terms of the three areas of lust. In each area, discuss how Christians can be in bondage to "the spirit of the age."

2
CULTURE AND WORLDLINESS

Y EARS AGO, AFTER SOME MONTHS of attending a church in Winnipeg, Lorrie and I applied for membership. To our surprise and chagrin we were informed that on the basis of our faulty doctrine we were being turned down. The church was pre-mil/pre-trib and because we couldn't say for sure that we were, our eschatology was condemned.

The church's leaders were also committed to a once-saved-never-lost statement. Lorrie and I were, too, but we admitted to some uncertainty as to the thrust of Hebrews 6 (a matter which has since become more settled in our minds, along Calvinist lines). Hence (apparently) the tea-cup storm.

The crisis was intensely painful all around. We had many dear friends in the church, some of whom had shown us exceptional kindness, and none of whom wanted us to leave. I think they must have felt we were being merely stubborn in not signing that doctrinal statement.

But a power struggle was going on. In retrospect, I can recognize that I was a threat to certain people in leadership. However, it was not until years later that the real reason for their reaction became apparent.

The real issue (I am now convinced) had to do with worldliness rather than with Bible doctrine. Shortly before the storm erupted I had been asked to give a Sunday evening address (now long-forgotten, I am sure) on the subject. Something vague had been said to me about "our young people," that is to say, the young people in the church. I had only been half listening at the time and had not grasped that the parents of teenagers in the church were worried about the behavior of their adolescent and young adult sons and daughters. So in my naiveté I gave a heart-felt address on 1 John 2:15-17, "Do not love the world nor the things that are in the world. . . ." I pointed out that worldliness, in John's view, seems to go much deeper than contemporary evangelical views and to emphasize something different from *worldliness* as we commonly use the word. One can avoid the movies and beer parties and still harbor worldly bitterness and pride. We can be cigarette-free, but untruthful, total abstainers, but gossipers, modest in dress, but acquisitive.

While I had no intention of promoting dancing, drinking, lurid make-up, card-playing, gambling, smoking, or movie-going, I was careful to point out that the heart of worldliness has more to do with carnality, possessiveness, jealousy, pursuit of beautiful material objects, pride, and snobbery than with the more traditional evangelical taboos. But (and this is where I got myself into hot water) without my being aware of it, my words were seen as sword thrusts at the values of the middle class parents rather than at the habits of their movie-going children. I doubt that the parents would now admit this, though I discovered (years later) that the address had aroused indignation and resentment in the very people who had asked me to give it, including church leaders, who from then on viewed me as dangerously unsound in my doctrine.

Jesus once warned about the Pharisees because they were "blind leaders of the blind" (Matt. 15:16), pointing out that leader and follower alike would fall into the ditch. The moral blindness which afflicts the church today is in part the result of church leaders such as these who condemn sins their hearers never commit while ignoring other sins that they and their congregations alike are guilty of.

What is worldliness? When John uses the term *the world*, to what does he refer? To what extent have Christians in the twentieth century been polluted by the spirit of the age?

The negative definition: Christians don't
The questions are of incalculable importance. I think of a conversation with my *batman* (an armed forces term for a personal servant) in the country once known as Ceylon. Timidly he asked my friend and me one morning: "Excuse me, sirs, but are you Christians?" We said we were

and asked him what prompted his question.

"Well, sirs, you don't smoke."

"Is that all?"

"No, sirs. Oh no. You don't seem to drink either, or dance, or go to parties."

I felt defeated. Did he (and the rest of the world, and worst of all, we Christians) perceive godliness in negative terms only? Were we in fact lacking in love, peace, joy, and other positive aspects of holiness? Had my attendant failed to see any of these spiritual fruits in our lives? He, like all of us, seemed to be aware that there *should* be visible differences between Christians and non-Christians; the two should be clearly distinguishable. "By their fruit you will recognize them," Jesus once declared, speaking of both true and false disciples (Matt. 7:17-20 NIV). My Ceylonese interrogator was certainly aware that the area of difference lay with what Christians didn't do, and possibly (though this was something we never found out) that the difference also concerned positive attitudes and actions which showed clearly who was and who was not a follower of Jesus. Christian behavior should be marked by both dos and don'ts, more, I hope, by the former than the latter. But from the first century on, confusion and disagreement have arisen both within and without the church as to what these dos and don'ts are.

Our shifting standards
Nowadays we think in a different framework from that of the apostle John. Some of us are more inclined to think in terms of culture and its influence on Christianity. The term *worldliness* has assumed narrower connotations than John had in mind. Later on we can take a

closer look at what John meant by his expression *the world.*

But if we think in twentieth century categories for a moment, one or two basic issues will come into focus. By culture I do not refer to such phenomena as our familiarity with Bach, modern poetry, and art, but to the patterns of behavior that characterize different societies. Primitive tribes have cultures of their own, and in the western hemisphere it is important to people from Europe (or Latin America or the Orient) to preserve their ethnic traditions and their way of life. They are deeply concerned that their children not lose their cultural heritage.

In my part of Canada we talk about the Mennonite culture, Ukrainian culture, French culture, and many others. Every year in Winnipeg, groups whose roots were torn from many nations sponsor an event called Folklorama. All over the city there are pavilions reflecting the cooking, the music, the arts, and crafts from nearly forty areas of the world. You can buy a passport for $12.50 which entitles you to enter each pavilion at least once ("immigration officials" stamp your passport to show which pavilions you have visited). It is one of Winnipeg's largest and most exciting events. Old people and young try to visit as many pavilions as they can each night, sampling the cooking and baking, admiring and often buying craft work, listening to the music and enjoying the performance of traditional dance forms.

We speak in Canada of our cultural mosaic and I imagine that the variety of cultures is reflected not only here in North America but in all parts of the English-speaking world.

Christian faith and cultural patterns

The critical question for the Christian then becomes: To what extent should my Christian faith incorporate cultural values? To what extent and in what ways can I and should I differ from my culture? Where do Christ and my culture blend naturally? Where do they conflict?

It is sometimes easier to see the problems when we translate them into cultures other than our own. Missionaries, since the inception of the modern missionary movement, and particularly since World War II, have been giving increasing thought to the degree to which a presentation of the gospel should reflect the missionary's own culture and values. There is an increasing awareness that we have been presenting a mixture: the gospel plus our national values and idiosyncrasies.

Converts to Christianity sometimes unthinkingly pick up bits of the missionary's culture even when the missionary tries conscientiously to avoid a culturalized version of the Good News. I was interested and amused to observe some years ago that Ayore women in Bolivia at that time all wanted dresses with a square neckline. Apparently some of the early women missionaries wore that style of dress, and the square neckline had somehow become part of what was recognized as godly apparel.

Eugene Nida drew attention to many of these issues in his book *Customs & Cultures: Anthropology for Christian Missions* (Wm. Carey Lib., 1975) and to the problems that arise, even in Bible translations, when culture is disregarded or lost sight of. I remember my amusement on learning of the problem of translating the verb *to kiss* and the noun *a kiss* into an African tribal language. The tribe had no such practice as kissing and the informant could not quite grasp what was meant from the missionary's descriptions of it. When the missionary tried to demonstrate by making kissing noises, the informant said (in his tribal language) "Ah, I see what you mean. That is what we call *sucking*." In desperation the missionary tried again: "What do you do to your wife when you want her to know how much you love her?" With a roguish smile the informant confided, "Try rubbing her elbow!"

Is there something peculiarly Christian about a kiss? Or is kissing merely a culturally conditioned mode of expressing affection? Ought the tribe to quit rubbing elbows and kiss in the Judeo-Christian fashion to be *real* Christians? Certainly the difference between Christians and other tribal members might show up in the matter of elbow-rubbing, but I think most of us would agree that learning to kiss instead of to rub elbows would be a very inadequate way of demonstrating Christian distinctiveness.

On the other hand, it is quite possible that some missionaries inflate the issue of cultural integrity beyond its real importance. One missionary I know of did not hesitate to speak authoritatively, as part of her message on certain purely cultural matters. Dead people, she declared firmly, should not be hung on trees to be eaten by vultures but should be buried six feet under, in true Christian style. But the outpouring of the Holy Spirit associated with her ministry, the enduring quality of the many churches she founded, and the unquestionable godliness of the church members in her area made her cultural transgressions seem unimportant.

Culture—a red herring?
The issue of Christianity and culture would merely pro-

33

vide a provocative and interesting topic for armchair discussion were it not that all cultures—yours, mine and everybody else's—reflect both evil and good. Though human behavior patterns trace their source back to creation and God and were labelled "good" by him, all have since been molded in part by Satan, by the Fall, by the universal curse of the Almighty. At different points, all culture patterns become battlegrounds between the power of darkness and the power of light. And it seems to me that the Enemy's most diabolical strategem consists of focusing our attention and energy on cultural trivia while blinding us to our grave offences against God. We justify our distorted views of holiness by proof texts which prove nothing. Like the Pharisees whom Jesus addressed in Matthew 23:24, we strain at gnats and swallow camels. I believe I am not alone in feeling that a new pharisaism, a new and increasingly deadly worldliness, has affected evangelical Christianity throughout the English-speaking world.

The Enemy has yet another tactic. His policy is clearly one of "divide and conquer." He seeks always and everywhere to set the followers of Christ one against another. Jesus, in his high-priestly prayer, besought the Father that the same quality of one-ness that is seen to characterize Father, Son, and Spirit might also characterize Christian people.

It was never for uniformity, nor even for organizational cohesiveness, that Jesus prayed. His concern was for the formation of harmonious relationships, springing from our common love of God, our common zeal to serve and honor him, and our common gratitude to our Redeemer.

Yet various groups among us are divided over cultural gnats and camels. Satan subtly turns the cultural differences that naturally distinguish us from one another into a source of mutual suspicion and criticism and even a source of pride.

Thus, when I meet for prayer with some local charismatic groups, I may feel ill at ease as scores of hands are raised and the chorus of "Jesus, Jesus, Jee-zus" swells and falls along with "Yes, Jesus. Precious Jesus. Amen, Lord." I grow uncomfortable not because there is anything doctrinally wrong with their exuberant worship but because I am a reserved Englishman and however hard I try I cannot, at this point in my life, shed all my cultural inhibitions. Many charismatics, on the other hand, are still members of churches with strictly liturgical worship patterns, though others have abandoned such churches because the liturgy seems too restrictive for them. Yet it is not the use of liturgy that hinders the freedom of the Holy Spirit so much as its abuse. Too often words and phrases that are not only beautiful, but also strong and magnificent and biblical vehicles of spiritual praise and adoration, are mechanically parroted and their meaning disregarded. It is easier to understand the appeal of free and spontaneous worship in such a context.

But it is precisely at this point, concerning the style of worship, that charismatics and noncharismatics may become defensive of themselves and zealous converters of others. I am glad that my charismatic friends have the liberty to shed some unnecessary inhibitions, but I am less than certain that their freedom is a sign of godliness and my own reserve an evidence of ungodliness.

Years ago I found myself in a plane sitting between

two Mennonites, one of them associated with the Holdeman conference and the other with the Mennonite Brethren (MB) conference. The MB Mennonite was the oldest of the three of us and was inclined to needle his fellow anabaptist. This was interesting to me—especially since the MB man asked questions I would never have dared to ask.

The Holdeman pastor was from Texas, on his way to visit Manitoba to participate in a series of revival meetings. He was gentle, courteous, thin, and neatly dressed. He wore a dark suit, no tie, had short hair and a carefully trimmed beard. The MB man was inclined to obesity, wore a tie, but was clean shaven and more jocular and talkative than the Holdeman brother.

We all had to change planes at one point and decided to eat together in the airport restaurant, where a straining-of-gnats conversation soon got underway. Why did the Holdeman brother wear no tie? Gravely he informed us that to follow the world's fashions slavishly was to give way to a temptation to vanity. Why the beard? Because God had made man so; man was different from woman. Then why trim the beard? Because there should be moderation in all things and because untidiness was no virtue. (Certainly he looked handsome with his beard!)

The MB man was attacking and the Holdeman pastor courteously defending while I held my breath. Somehow I liked the Holdeman guy and was embarrassed by the MB man's half-jocular, half-serious ribbing. At one point I became acutely conscious of the two gold rings on my left fourth finger (one wedding ring, almost worn out, and a second to make up for it!). Nobody said anything but the Holdeman brother glanced at them and then looked away quickly. For him, jewelry of all forms was out.

Who ordered the wine? I'm sure I didn't and I'm even more sure the Holdeman didn't. I can't even remember whether I drank from my glass. But I distinctly remember that it added the sense of a new element of strain around the table.

I also remember that we did not talk about the glory of Christ, nor about the abundant grace of God to a world of sinful rebels. We shared nothing about our personal weaknesses and needs, nor did we testify to God's help in those same needs. And though I have no proof of it, I sensed that the Holdeman pastor, gracious though he was, felt a moral superiority over both of us, and that the MB man was convinced that the Holdeman alone was swallowing camels and straining at gnats. I was relieved when, on boarding our next plane, we dropped our preoccupation with behavioral minutiae. Though I asked for more details about the Holdeman's meetings and promised to pray for him, I was uneasily aware that I was really proffering an olive branch rather than demonstrating genuine concern. Since that time, terrible tragedy has overtaken the Manitoba Holdeman brethren, but that is another story, except to note that owning television sets and cars were among the "gnats" that brought denunciation and excommunication among them, dividing families and creating very great pain.

Questions for Study and Discussion

1. Write a definition of worldliness that reflects common evangelical taboos today. Now write a definition of worldliness based on 1 John 2:15-17. Discuss how and why these two definitions differ.

2. What sins do most of today's church-goers focus on? What sins are they blind to? Be specific.

3. To what extent and in what ways should Christians differ from their culture?

4. Identify elements of Christian faith and life that are transcultural.

5. Read Matthew 23:24 and discuss how deeply pharisaism afflicts the church today.

6. Describe some of Satan's current, destructive strategies against the church.

3

ON STRAINING
AT GNATS

AUGUSTINE (WHOM NEVER HAVING MET, I still love)
wound up as the celibate bishop of Hippo in North
Africa. If I understand the record correctly, he remained
celibate because his sexual weaknesses were such that for
him sexual joys had to be given up entirely, or they would
have made him their slave.

I have faced a problem like that, not with sex, but with
books. With a lightened heart I once had to give up my
prized, private collection of English classics of the romantic era (including some early editions) which had come
between me and my Lord. It was a struggle, but God
freed me. For a number of years it meant literary abstinence on my part. But in his grace he has restored to me,

as a servant, the thing that once threatened to be my master.

Slavery or self-denial?

There is no question in my mind that being not of the world will involve for all of us, at different points, self-denial. I must never become a slave of anyone or anything but Jesus. This means that behavioral changes may be called for at the point of my greatest weakness.

But note. The thing given up may differ for each of us. Moreover the abstinence is common sense, not virtue. And here we open up a can of worms, for we must come to grips with principles of right and wrong, describe erroneous views of what constitutes holiness, and point out the ways by which God brings true holiness into our lives.

Think of some current "Christian laws."

Thou shalt not smoke.

Thou shalt not drink alcohol.

Thou shalt not dress too fashionably.

Thou shalt not buy season tickets to the ballet.

Down the ages, unworldliness has consisted of giving up, not only sinful, but also neutral or even good and right things. This has had a number of consequences, some amusing and others serious. One amusing consequence is that we may tend to equate separation from the world with avoiding enjoyable activities—things we like —and as a consequence regarding as holy many things we actively dislike. This is one of the Devil's more sadistic jokes.

A graver consequence is that we turn unworldliness into a legalistic merit system. Though we may affirm that we do not smoke because we do not wish to defile the temple of the Holy Spirit (our bodies) and that we go to church three times on Sunday because we love Jesus and not as a "good work," our hearts deceive us. The feelings of deprivation or boredom or martyrdom with which we fulfill these requirements betray us.

Then there's guilt, the guilt we experience when we fail to keep up with our self-imposed good works, which also betrays us. For two weeks in a row we have failed to attend the Wednesday night prayer meeting and we find ourselves compelled to explain our reasons at length to the pastor's wife. We pledged (in a moment of enthusiasm) to support a short-term missionary from our congregation and when inflation and other financial stresses make it difficult or impossible to fulfill our pledge, we feel again the pangs of frustration and guilt.

Worst of all, our pride in our dos and don'ts makes us self-righteous. Our legalism condemns us before God while it enslaves our own consciences. We are proud of having no television set in our home and guilty because we enjoy watching it at the neighbor's house.

It is important that I make myself clear. Am I saying that, once justified through the grace of God and the blood of Christ, we may indulge in sin? Am I condoning habits like smoking and drinking? I neither condone nor condemn either. There are practical, common-sense reasons for avoiding both.

Smoking impairs health, producing cancer, chronic obstructive lung disease, and possibly coronary artery disease. It is an expensive habit and induces addiction, which results in even greater expense and destruction of the body. (It's easy for me to point out these problems; I

41

am a nonsmoker.) Again, my smoking could stumble some brother or sister for whom such indulgence would be sin, because of a lack of understanding and a weak conscience.

So is smoking *right* or *wrong*? It cannot be both, but it may be neither. I am glad that Dutch Reformed pastors in Holland can enjoy smoking their pipes, although I hope they are aware of some of the health hazards of doing so. I am also glad when I see friends who have the guts to kick the smoking habit, as a matter of health and good sense. Perhaps you think I am talking out of both sides of my mouth. Not at all. Without realizing what we are doing, we have set up systems of unworldliness that depend on the dos and don'ts and taboos we impose on one another. We were ransomed from sin by God so that we might become free, free from both the penalty and the power of sin. But having been freed we may have led our Christian brothers and sisters back into new forms of bondage.

And drinking? A drunkard is not free. To be freed in Christ he needs both forgiveness and deliverance. And deliverance from drunkenness may well mean, for him, to become a permanent, total abstainer. For the drunkard, to drink is to tempt God, and to tempt God is to sin. There is no *virtue* in his being a total abstainer rather than a moderate drinker. But total abstention is both deliverance from slavery and plain common sense for him.

Again, a nondrinker (or a careful and moderate drinker) might also decide to abstain totally. In view of the massive promotion of alcoholic beverages and the rising crime and accident rate from increased alcohol consumption, Christians may do well to avoid buying and using wine or liquor in order to avoid promoting the consumption of a chemical which is certainly harmful, at the present time, to society as a whole. Yet let not those who abstain condemn those who don't. By his own Master each will be judged, whether it be he who is free to partake or he who is freed from partaking.

Jesus had a sense of humor. (I am grateful to Elton Trueblood for pointing this out.) Some of the metaphors Jesus used are brilliantly funny. At one point he spoke of "straining at gnats" (on which most of us have coughed and choked at some point) and "swallowing camels" (which none of us has ever attempted). It was his witty, hyperbolic way of making an ethical point. We strain at gnats. That is, we worry over movie-going, dancing or TV-watching, and a host of other minor issues (though there is nothing wrong with concern over any of these things).

But we also swallow camels. For example, we (or people richer than we) may make a million bucks in a shady deal—a deal which exploits the poor or makes the dealer rich at the expense of someone else's pain and loss. As a result, the dealer gets elected to the church board, where rich individuals are an asset. And the same wheeler-dealer thunders at board meetings about the worldliness of TV. By all means let us denounce TV. Some of the shows on the tube are appalling and degrading. But dare he thunder whose own riches were gained by exploiting the poor? Such a man or woman has a beam in his or her eye, and has not only strained at a gnat but swallowed a camel.

Take a sixty-year-old maiden lady. Never in her life

has she drunk even a glass of sherry. She has never owned a TV set. She has never—oh but *never*—smoked a cigarette. She tithes religiously. Her hemlines are low and her neckline high. Her jewelry is anonymous. She attends the Wednesday night prayer meeting without fail.

Yet she gossips. She is self-righteous. The rumors she spreads about the church young people are not only inaccurate but damaging. She calls the pastor almost every day with some new and juicy bit of scandal. She is a strainer at the gnats of movies, TV, and dancing and a swallower of the camels of gossip, divisiveness, judgmentalism, and unkindness. And she will always be a frustrated, unhappy woman.

Once again, I am not advocating sherry, nor am I suggesting that it is commendable for you to skip the Wednesday night prayer meeting. But I am trying to give you an idea of what true worldliness is all about. It has to do with your heart and your motives before a holy God.

But even here I must be careful. I must never imply that even our most trivial actions are unimportant or that correct motives render any action sinless or holy. It is just that we cannot assess their virtue or their vice without taking into account our motives. How many self-righteous people I have known (bitter, unhappy people) who have grimly asserted their righteousness on the basis of dos and don'ts that are gnats, while they have swallowed the camels of pride, of bitterness, of legalism, and of rejection of all those whom the world calls sinners, drunks, prostitutes, and bums.

Drunks and prostitutes are certainly sinners. But usually they *know* they are sinners. Many are sinners in whose hearts the Holy Spirit has begun his work of conviction. But if, perhaps desperate for help, they walk into almost any evangelical church on Sunday morning (and some do), they end up sneaking away with a miserable feeling that they do not belong. Most people like that never show up for the same reason. Why? Because they *know* we strain at gnats and swallow camels, whereas Jesus, doing neither, met with sinners, ate and drank with them, sat with them, and freely and lovingly preached the gospel to them.

Too often we confuse separation from the world with pharisaism. Jesus upbraided the Pharisees for their close adherence to what they themselves called *the tradition of the elders* —human customs and rules they equated with holiness (as in Mark 7). So important were these traditions to the Pharisees that, perhaps without realizing what they were doing, they neglected God's weightier commandments (Matt. 23:23-24). We tend to regard Pharisees as evil men. Yet many of them were zealous guardians of the faith. They opposed the modernism of the Sadducees—those early liberals who denied the truth of Scriptural teaching about demons, angels, and the resurrection. Admittedly, the doctrine of the resurrection was not explicit in the Old Testament but, as Jesus pointed out, it was implied. As for angels, the Old Testament had much to say about them. To be fair to the Pharisees then, we should regard them as good fundamentalists, a group with whom they had much in common.

Yet Christ's condemnation of the Pharisees far exceeded anything he ever said about the Sadducees. Why? Because, knowing the Word of God and professing to honor it, they yet exalted their accumulated religious traditions above God's commands. "You have a fine way of rejecting the commandment of God, in order to keep your tradition," he told them (Mark 7:9 RSV). How often we do the same thing, not only in principle but literally. (There are some Christians who are complacent about their generosity to the Christian cause while dishonoring or neglecting their own parents.)

The serious sins

In what ways, then, should Christians differ from non-Christians? So far we have looked only at pride, bodily lusts, and materialism. But what is important in Scripture? Is God more concerned about some things than others? Or is all sin the same? Is it not true that except for our justification in Christ, the least sin would damn us all in God's sight?

It seems that distinctions must be made between serious and less serious sins. Lucifer's first sin was pride. Pride, falsehood, and oppressive violence are among the sins most objected to in the Old Testament. "There are six things the Lord hates, seven that are detestable to him: haughty eyes, a lying tongue, hands that shed innocent blood, a heart that devises wicked schemes, a false witness who pours out lies, feet that are quick to rush into evil and a man who stirs up dissension among brothers" (Prov. 6:16-19 NIV).

If we must categorize sin, looking for priorities, let us note the Scripture's thrust against pride, the first sin and the worst. God says, "I hate pride and arrogance, evil behavior, and perverse speech" (Prov. 8:13 NIV). The cruelty and unconscious pride as well as the chauvinism of the Pharisees was seen in their attitude to prostitution and sexual immorality. How great was their delight in dragging through the dust toward Jesus a woman caught in the act of adultery! A crowd of men and one cowering, terrified, shame-filled woman, possibly a victim of a lustful male. And where was he—her partner in fornication? Did they let him go? "Caught in the act," they were crowing, so certainly the man must have been part of the act (John 8:3-8).

Or again, think of the scorn of Simon as a sinful woman poured out her tears of gratitude at the feet of Jesus. Clearly the Master was not a prophet, reasoned Simon, or he would have discerned the kind of trash she was (not that one needs to be a prophet to spot a whore). Redemptive concern and love clearly had no part in Simon's thinking. That Jesus wanted to rescue the prostitute would have seemed incredible to him.

To the Pharisees, adultery was far worse than pride and I believe that as Christians we make the same mistake. We have similar values to those of the Pharisees.

As for falsehood I find, to my shame, that it is one of my greatest temptations. In my eagerness to please or impress, I exaggerate. My pride thus contributes to my tendency to be untruthful. I remember a psychiatrist who undertook part of my training laughing uproariously as a group of us sat around a table having coffee. "Oh, John," he said "surely you don't believe in a literal Adam and Eve!" I was ashamed (another result of pride) and too quickly replied in a way which implied that I *didn't* believe in the original pair. I lied. It was difficult for me (because of my pride) to go back to him later and confess to having lied about my beliefs. Yet in the mercy of God, it was that same psychiatrist who came to me later to request that if I were around when he died he would esteem it a kindness if I were to conduct his funeral service.

Were it not for the fact that the Spirit of God constantly prompts me, I would give way to pride and lying very frequently. Pride, lying and unkindness, or cruelty stand high on the list of the things God hates. If we would be different from the world we must learn humility, truthfulness, and kindness. Remember, the perpetrator of the seventh deadly sin in Proverbs is "he who stirs up dissension among brothers" (Prov. 6:19 NIV).

The cruelty can take many forms and may wear a cloak of piety. Some churches in the area where I now live insist that young married couples who have indulged in sex play before their wedding day stand up before the congregation and confess their sin—sin against God and the congregation. If they fail to do so, they are "disfellowshipped" and the reason for their excommunication is announced in their absence. I have no desire to defend sexual hanky-panky, but the church "discipline" I have described smacks more of smug cruelty than mercy, and panders to the self-righteous satisfaction of older and more sexually inhibited members of the congregation. Where the couple's wrong was primarily against God and each other, and did not damage the congregation as a whole, a more godly way to have handled the matter would have been to counsel and pray with the couple themselves, in private, with the goal of repentance and restoration to fellowship.

Silence is also a murderous weapon. We disapprove of

someone, or resent them, and so we turn our backs on them. For several years, one member of a church we attended studiously turned her back on my wife every time Lorrie greeted her. The lady would be warm and even effusive with me, but would walk away from Lorrie, leaving her with an outstretched but unshaken hand. Lorrie's attempts to discover the nature of the trouble were met with silence and a retreating figure striding purposefully toward the church door. God, in his mercy, resolved the problem after a couple of years. But the careless exclusion of humbler members of the church from socially successful cliques is a form of the same cruelty.

The ways of divisiveness and cruelty are endless—prayer meetings where some absent member is subtly damned by the subterfuge of a pseudo-spiritual prayer request. A great deal of Christian gossip begins with the phrase, "I think Anne needs our prayers...." Poor Anne usually has no idea what is going on. So we form ourselves into arrogantly pious cliques and sanctified parties ready to do battle for the Devil in the name of the Lord.

"Blessed are the poor in spirit," Jesus said, "for theirs is the kingdom of heaven" (Matt. 5:3). Poor in spirit? What on earth does that mean? (Someone to whom I spoke yesterday thought it meant depressed.) Others seem to think it refers to the inability to stand up for yourself because of a weak or passive character. For many years it was interpreted as material poverty, and therefore thought to refer to someone who kowtowed to the arrogant rich.

It means none of these things. To be poor in spirit means to recognize that I am morally and spiritually bankrupt. It means that I know I have no right to lift up my head—neither before man nor before God. I am a sinner. I am a hopeless and helpless failure. I have no rights before God. Recognizing my plight is the first step. The poor in spirit, then, are those who recognize their moral and spiritual poverty, and recognizing it, mourn.

Nor are the poverty of spirit and the mourning one-time events. Deep as is my understanding of God's saving grace to me, rejoice as I may in the once-for-all justification he has imparted to me, celebrate as I must my adoption into God's family, I can never forget my total moral bankruptcy apart from grace. And as, once again, I trip and fall, I mourn afresh, even though joy smiles through my tears. I mourn my offence in the face of his kindness, and as I mourn, he comforts me. "Blessed are the meek," Jesus continued; "for they shall inherit the earth" (Matt. 5:5). Not the proud. Not the arrogant. Not those who succeed in getting to the top in this world's game of King of the Mountain. The meek. Those who do not become defensive when they are told the truth about themselves. Those who do not laugh it off when they are criticized or snubbed, and who don't mind losing an argument. Those who know how to laugh at themselves, who have learned not to take themselves too seriously.

Motives and their fruit

"Blessed are those who hunger and thirst for righteousness," Jesus continued (Matt. 5:6 RSV), for not taking oneself seriously does not mean that one is unconcerned about holiness and truth. Indeed, those who know their spiritual and moral bankruptcy, and who are meek enough to acknowledge it, are the ones who most ardently crave righteousness both in themselves and in those around them. They are the pure in heart—that is to say, they have only one aim in life—to please God. With such an aim, each of us will be a peacemaker, bringing about the reconciliation between one neighbor and another, as a result of the reconciliation each of us as peacemakers has found with God.

This is what is meant by being a light in the darkness. It is what makes true Christians salty. It begins with the recognition of one's moral and spiritual bankruptcy, and is accompanied by grief over sin, and by humility and mercy.

Does this mean that sexual sin is unimportant, then, or that we may do whatever we wish, provided we hurt no one? By no means. It simply means that all morality arises out of our broken and constant acknowledgement of our need of God's mercy. Only then will our righteous behavior be superior to that of the Pharisees. Only then will our light shine in the darkness and our saltiness preserve the world from utter corruption.

Humanity's first mistake was to respond with pride instead of thankfulness (Rom. 1:21) and to assume that mankind is wise when in fact we are all fools. God allowed us to reap the foul consequences of our pride and folly; we became enslaved to perverted sexuality (Rom. 1:24-27), to covetous greed, malice, cruelty, and to other forms of evil behavior (Rom. 1:28-32). Many people view behavior as secondary, as a symptom, rather than a problem in itself. But behavior is important. To say that morality is concerned only with proper motives, or that so long as our hearts are right our actions do not matter, reflects a shallow, shortsighted view of man. A righteous heart produces righteous behavior just as a good tree produces healthy fruit, and is known for it. We are called upon to share Christ's mind (Phil. 2:5) and to have that form of humility that results in obedience to the point of death (Phil. 2:6-8). If anyone who reads these words feels that the standards taught by Jesus in the Sermon on the Mount were mere legalities of a kingdom age, let him read on into the Pauline Epistles. There he will find the same standards of behavior occupying a major part of every letter Paul wrote.

Having established the underlying principles—poverty of spirit, an everwillingness to mourn at the quickness with which I grieve my Redeemer, meekness (lack of defensiveness), truthfulness, openness, gentleness and kindness, the concern to bring about reconciliation among those whom God reconciled to himself, and endless and often-repeated gratitude to a God whose long-suffering and mercy can never be repaid—principles that enable us to be freed from worldly lusts, let us look at some other areas of misunderstanding before we deal with specific sins and failures.

Questions for Study and Discussion

1. Think of an area in your life which might threaten your own freedom in Christ. What can you do to guard against slavery to this habit or tendency?

2. List some "gnats" that Christians strain at.

3. List some of the "camels" that Christians swallow.

4. How did Jesus avoid both gnats and camels?

5. Are some sins more serious than others? What sins does the Bible seem to indicate are most serious in God's eyes?

6. Describe the relationship between behavior and motivation. Which comes first? Discuss their relative importance.

4

SLAVERY—
MODERN STYLE

I AM WRITING WHILE SITTING in a hotel room. Lorrie and I, very weary from overwork, are trying to relax and recover. A day or so ago we met a delightful couple about ten years younger than we. These friends (who I will call Kevin and Cathy) are staying at the same hotel. Kevin is a Nova Scotia fisherman. So far as we know, they are not active Christians.

"Let's give them a call," Lorrie says suddenly. So we do. "Yes, sure we'd love to come up and join you," Kevin responds cheerfully. The day is cold and cloudy. "We're just finishing a game of cards."

Cards? There we go again. Suddenly it occurs to me that the Devil has sold us a stereotype about worldliness.

Why do many Christians still feel acutely uncomfortable about playing cards? (I understand there are some excellent card games.)

The discomfort, I suppose, arises from the association of cards with gambling. If you never play cards you are less likely to gamble. Cards and gambling are "worldly." They fit neatly into our stereotype of worldliness.

Forgive me if I repeat myself—maybe you're getting tired of it—but just for the record I am not, repeat *not*, trying to entice you to play cards and gamble. We're into the gnats and camels thing again, mostly it's still the gnats (which were never meant to be swallowed, remember?). Later we'll get around to camels.

The hotels around here (we're in the Bahamas) are cluttered with casinos—great carpeted halls lit by massive chandeliers and crowded with thrill seekers, some in evening dress, others wearing whatever they fancy. (The only things you're not allowed to wear are T-shirts and shorts.)

About half the vast gambling area is filled with one-armed bandits—machines into which you put quarters before pulling the lever. The wheels spin around and come to a stop. Then you put another quarter in, pull the lever again (the lever is the *arm* of the one-armed bandit) and set the wheels spinning afresh. Once in a while a bell will ring and then the bandit will vomit a belly-full of quarters into the metal receiver below its mouth. Or it may cough up only half a dozen. Everything depends on the combination that shows up, randomly, from the spinning of the wheels.

The rest of the hall is filled with card tables, roulette tables, baccarat tables, the wheel of fortune, and others that in my ignorance I can neither recognize nor understand. The noise is constant. Jingling quarters from the one-armed bandits. Shouts of joy. Voices raised in the occasional quarrel.

Some tables are crowded with excited onlookers. Others are almost deserted. A couple of women wearing sequined evening dresses are watching the black croupier, and he them. All three faces are bored, sullen, world-weary. The women take plastic colored chips from the piles lying beside them. They place some in the middle of numbered squares, and others at the point where four, numbered squares intersect. The ball spins giddily in the channel around the spinning roulette wheel, then, as it slows, it begins to dance among the numbers of the wheel. Slowly it comes to rest. Neither of the women has chosen the lucky number. The attendant reaches out with a long handled instrument and sweeps the colored chips into a container. Immediately the women lay more chips out.

Gambling. The epitome of worldliness?

Let us examine the faces of the people at play. Many of them are nothing like the two women. They are smiling. If you talk to them you find out that most of them are there for fun. "Did you win anything?" you may ask. "Nah—not a thing!" laughs a red faced man. "It took me all evening to use up my ten bucks—but I enjoyed it." His wife adds eagerly "He only gave me five bucks to spend, and look!" She holds up two paper cups filled to the brim with quarters. "She always wins," says her husband, shaking his head and laughing again. These are the people who "know when to quit," whether they win or lose.

Gradually you become aware that there are two kinds

of people there. There are those who enjoy spending money playing a game, and who stop either when their limit is reached, or else when they "hit the jackpot." Win or lose, they are just having fun. Win or lose, they are under no inner compulsion to go on. They are content to "have a little fling." But others are in more serious difficulty—the ones who borrow money to gamble, and the occasional men and women who take their own lives after losing.

One Canadian lady we met spends hours and hours there. She can't quit. Last night she won several hundred dollars—but she couldn't stop playing and slowly lost them all. She is part of a crowd of addicts. For them, gambling is a desperate business, often the cause of violence or even murder. The attendants who run the gaming tables have a difficult and demanding job. Day and night they switch (forty minutes on, twenty minutes off) but even so, the tension they are under is so overwhelming that every month they are flown to Miami, some to rest, others for psychiatric help. The casino management foots the bill. And it can afford to, for casinos make big money. Many are Mafia-run and most have connections with the underworld of crime and corruption.

Why have I spent so much time describing a gambling casino? Partly because few Christians have ever been in one, partly to point out the curious parallel between gambling and alcohol. Most people who drink alcohol, either with a meal or "socially," are under no compulsion to escalate their drinking pattern until it is more or less continuous. They learn fairly early in life that the hangovers that follow their bouts of drunkenness are not worth the "fun" of being intoxicated, and they acquire the ability to say "No. Thank you." when they have reached what they recognize is their limit.

But others cannot stop. However often they resolve to control their drinking, and no matter what its consequences (broken homes, accidents, lost jobs, poverty), they are compelled to drink and drink again, often as an escape from these very problems. We call them *problem drinkers* and alcoholics. And gambling is to problem gamblers what alcohol is to alcoholics. They *mean* to quit, but they cannot. Instead, like alcoholics, they begin to deceive themselves—telling themselves that they have no problem, that their system is bound to work soon and will win them a fortune in the end.

Let us consider how the Christian church developed its horror of drinking and gambling. A hundred years ago, gamblers and drunks were literally *saved*, by a gracious God, from ruining their lives in these destructive ways. Very understandably, they taught their children to avoid the habits that had previously enslaved them. But gradually, righteousness and holiness became more a matter of staying out of saloons and brothels, more a gnat and camel issue, a negative, than the development of a strong, inner virtue, or the reflection of shining holiness of Christ, who is Lord in the life.

In Scripture, the nearest anyone came to gambling was the "casting of lots." Roman soldiers cast lots over Jesus' cloak; the apostles cast lots to decide on a replacement for Judas. The Old Testament refers again and again to decisions based on casting lots, a method approved by God in his instructions to his people, and there is never any suggestion that this form of gambling was, in itself, sinful, for "the lot is cast into the lap, but the decision is wholly from the Lord" (Prov. 16:33).

But we must not fall into the trap of saying that the Scripture's silence on certain issues means that anything goes, or that such silence leaves us free to do as we please. Take alcohol, for example. In England, during the industrial revolution, French brandy was heavily taxed and gin became the poor man's way of getting drunk. Work was hard, pay was poor, and life was miserable, so alcoholism increased by leaps and bounds. Hogarth, the English artist, recorded bizarre scenes of drunken depravity in his series, *The Rake's Progress.* Women and children drank as much as men. Babies would carelessly be dropped and maimed or accidentally killed by their drunken mothers.

When William Booth and his Salvation Army began its work, drunkenness abounded. To be converted and to join the Salvation Army meant to quit gin and all forms of alcohol. And the Salvation Army was right. Even moderate drinking was rightly condemned. In such an environment the Christian's only proper course of action lay in total abstinence.

Now, though the Bible nowhere *commands* such absolute abstinence, who can doubt that in these circumstances the Salvation Army made a right decision?

Should we then fault southern Italians or Argentine Christians (of Brethren Assemblies) for taking wine with their meals in conformity to long-standing custom? Common sense demands that certain habits, at critical points in social development, call for a re-evaluation of right and wrong. For instance, it would seem logical to suggest that the more alcoholism increases, the more the church should condemn its use and abuse.

Or take a clearer example. When China Inland Missionaries first penetrated inland China, opium was a curse. How could the mission and its converts (among them that great scholar and antiopium campaigner, Pastor Hsi) do anything but forthrightly condemn the use of opium? "Everything is permissible for me," says Paul, quoting a popular saying, "but not everything is beneficial" (1 Cor. 10:23). 'Everything is permissible for me, *but I will not be mastered by anything,* and opium was an unrelenting taskmaster to almost everyone who used it.

What comments then can we make? First that cards or gambling are for some people what alcohol, or drugs, are for others—a deadly and desperate disease which is responsible for ruining and breaking up countless families. Second, to gamble in a casino is to pour money into the bank accounts of wealthy casino owners (often criminals) whose craving for money and power drives them to exploit two kinds of people—the addicted, compulsive gambler and the pleasure-seeking tourist who doesn't mind losing or winning a few dollars as part of his holiday fun.

Around the casinos and under the same roofs are bars, restaurants, and lounges, offering refreshments of differing qualities and prices. Here and there in this environment, expensive prostitutes attach themselves to gamblers and egg them on. Some of the sicker gamblers may play for three or four days straight without ever going to bed.

Would Jesus have entered a casino? Certainly he is concerned about the people who go there today. He made it clear that those who are well do not need a physician, but those who are sick, and that he did not come to call the righteous, but sinners to repentance. It seems clear that the one who ate and drank with publicans and sinners would not have hesitated to conduct a search-and-rescue mission in a casino, or saloon, or house of ill fame.

Somewhere in our minds we have developed a stereotype, a caricature, not only of sin but of worldliness. It concerns the pursuit of pleasure and of what, for some people, are "dangerous" forms of pleasure. A song I once heard reminds me of the stereotype—"cigarettes and whiskey and wild, wild women." The empty and vain pursuit of pleasure. Hedonism with its alluring but empty promises. The world pursues these things. The church is at present in relatively little danger of being like the world in its gambling, cards, drunkenness, or in cigarettes and whiskey and wild, wild women. A few Christians perhaps, but not a significant number.

But think for a moment. The world is full of other people who, without knowing God, never gamble, never drink, do not smoke, pay their way in life, and bring up their children to be good citizens. Ought Christians to be different from *these* respectable people? And if so, how? An evening of fun in a gambling casino, or an evening playing cards with friends (we didn't play with Kevin and Cathy—we don't *know* any card games) may not be sin. It may not even be worldly, even though these activities conform to our stereotype of worldliness. To feel we are virtuous because we never go to casinos is to choke on a gnat (and please remember—I don't want you to start swallowing gnats).

Questions for Study and Discussion

1. Give brief personality profiles of two kinds of gamblers. What separates them?

2. For what reasons does the church condemn gambling?

3. What does the Bible have to say about gambling?

4. Discuss what the habits of compulsive gambling, drinking, and drug addiction have in common.

5. Is pleasure a valid pursuit for the Christian? Does pleasure, in itself, ever satisfy? Why or why not?

6. In light of the content of this chapter, what should be the Christian's attitude toward gambling and drinking?

5

TUNED IN AND TURNED ON

"**S**EX AND DRUGS AND ROCK 'N ROLL are all my body needs."

Such is the theme of a modern song that echoes the feelings of many people under thirty. I suppose it represents the younger set's version of their great-grandparents' song, "Cigarettes and Whiskey and Wild, Wild Women."

I realize I must be cautious in writing about rock and drugs, the subjects of this chapter. (Sex will be discussed later.) I once sat with my second son in the front of our car listening to the radio as he tried for an hour or so to teach me to discern the differences between good rock and bad rock, hard rock, and acid rock. The distinctions were clear to him, but though I could tell that they represented different kinds of noise, their subtleties were lost on me. On that particular day I couldn't even distinguish the words. My ear was too old. I belonged to a different generation. I was neither tuned in nor turned on.

The music

Many Christians see rock as unmitigated evil. Its heavy beat, reminiscent of the orgiastic rituals of tribal magic, is perceived as the Devil's personal brand of music. They could be right, but personally I cannot be dogmatic. Indeed, I am inclined to doubt so broad a generalization. As I listened with Kevin there were occasional snatches of sound which were beautiful and some were reminiscent of Bach. But is even Bach's music spiritual, in any sense?

By what criteria do we measure the morality of sounds and rhythm? When I was a boy the same things that are now being said about rock were being said about jazz. Yet now jazz has become respectable. Some of my Christian friends, whose integrity and spiritual depth I do not question, have record collections of jazz in which they find great enjoyment. Jazz is played on those FM stations that major in classical music. Is Mozart spiritual? Beethoven rebellious and carnal? Mendelssohn romantic? How can you tell? Are there criteria more valid and less subjective than personal taste by which we can pigeonhole our music?

I must make a distinction, of course, between music and the lyrics that go with it. But if we consider the sounds and rhythm alone I believe there is a lot to be said for the moral neutrality of any music. Certainly, if I had to pick between subdued, low-volume rock and some of the experimental work of "serious" composers of the seventies, with their taped collages of industrial and street sounds, their dissonances, machinery clankings and grindings, I think I would prefer rock. Again, whenever I have discussed the matter with my friend William Aide, a warm-hearted Christian who has taught music history for years at the University of Manitoba and at a couple of Ontario universities (and who is also an outstanding concert pianist), I have been assured that any morality attached to music arises solely from the associations we bring to it. Sentimental music is sentimental because we have learned to associate it with sentimental themes. Martial music is the kind of music we associate with the rhythm of marching soldiers. The Reformation hymn, *A Mighty Fortress,* was written to the music of a slightly bawdy tavern song in Luther's day, but now we associate the music only with majesty and triumph.

Should Christ postpone his return until the year two thousand fifty, it is possible that some elderly stick-in-the-muds will be singing God's praises to the rhythms of rock music, which will be, by then, held in contempt by the current crop of teen-agers.

The lyrics

Again, my knowledge is fragmentary. I have listened to disgusting obscenity (even in the bookstore of a Christian college where for several minutes I listened to a song whose pulsing theme was "Do it, do it, do it, do it . . ."—an explicit reference to copulation), have been urged to be kind to the Devil, and have heard enough to recognize that many of the lyrics either promote Dionysian revelry or something even more sinister. I also know that the words of some rock songs can have a disastrous influence on young people. My own son handed a pile of records to me with the words, "Get rid of these for me, Dad. They have a dreadful effect on me."

Yet I have also heard a yearning, the heart cry of a lost and groping generation. It comes through in some of the songs of the Beatles. It is noticeable in Bob Dylan's progress from his early search for meaning in life to the radical change of heart which was so apparent in his album *Slow Train Coming*. Personally, I dislike Dylan's nasal voice and find his music difficult to listen to, but I cannot question the reality that he searched till he was found by the very God who had placed those longings in his heart.

The drugs

I know a little more about drugs from my psychiatric work. I have had to deal with young men and women whose brains have been permanently damaged by glue and gasoline sniffing, by toxic mixtures passed off in the street as heroin or L.S.D. but laced with far more dangerous chemicals. I have also known the frustration of trying to sort out whether psychotic youngsters suffer from early schizophrenia precipitated by drug use, or merely from a temporary drug psychosis from which they will recover. What appalls me most of all is the knowledge that young grade-school children are being damaged by the use of purer and more potent forms of *cannabis* (the active ingredient in marijuana) than older teenagers and young adults ever faced when they were in high school. The result, it is now clear, is an irreversible lag in the development of their central nervous systems, and in their ability to relate either to their peers or to adults.

The anxiety of parents is thoroughly justified, as is the opposition of police and of Christian groups to the growing traffic in such drugs. The younger generation, however, point out with some validity that their parents use tranquilizers, which can also be harmful. I am appalled in my work by the number of patients I come across who have been taking minor tranquilizers for years. But how has such widespread drug use arisen? Clearly there are many factors. Mass communication that links young people and their culture patterns all over the Western world. Pharmaceutical companies that promote addicting hypnotics as well as healing antipsychotic medications. The ease and increase of international travel that makes possible a wide drug distribution by means of many agents. The greed of Mafia-like organizations for illicit profits—these and many other factors are all significant.

But why are young people so vulnerable? It seems a long time now since the hippies with their eccentric clothing, their long hair, their promiscuity, and their preaching of peace (along with their open defiance of their parents' materialism), aroused those same parents to anger. From this counter-culture movement arose religious movements, some evil and satanic, but others healthy and helpful. The *Jesus People* movement is one example.

What responsibility does the church in the West have for the off-beat mass movements affecting the younger generation to this very day? Are the youngsters' charges true? Have not we, the Western church, too readily identified ourselves with the goals of a materialistic, sterile, and technological society? Do we not see a progressive rise in the Gross National Product as the greatest good? Do we not worship bigness, whether in churches, in banks, or in business corporations? And is it not also true that bigness and technology degrade human labor, rob human beings of meaning, identity, and natural creativity? Humankind has become the victim of technology. Why is it that, in Detroit, psychologists employed by the auto industries are forever having to invent ways to help auto workers feel self-esteem?

In his excellent booklet, *The Age of Plenty,* E. F. Schumacher writes, "The future of industrial, technological society must be a future in which every man and woman, even 'the least among my brethren' can be *persons,* can see themselves and be seen by their children as real people, not as cogs in vast machines and gap-fillers in automated processes employed solely because, occasionally, the human machine is calculated to be a cheaper 'means of production' than a mindless device."

The church has embraced not only the values of a production-oriented technological society, but the technology itself. We use computerized typewriters to print out "personal" letters to donors and would-be donors. And the wider our television networks become, the more our gospel becomes an impersonal affair (in spite of the armies of telephone counselors) distanced by technology from the glazed-eyed television watcher.

The young people turn to sex, drugs and rock 'n roll partly, however foolishly, to find personal meaning and reality. They see us more clearly than we see ourselves. Like the society we are a part of, we scramble madly in pursuit of suburban houses, financial security, larger and better cars. We link our well-being to the G.N.P. We profess to believe in spiritual realities, but we act as though the material and our position in human society are all that matter. Our lives are unreal. I do not know whether Schumacher is right in urging us to pursue smallness, simplicity, capital saving, and non-violence (in industrial and farming processes). I do know that so long as we continue on our present course we will grow ever more alienated from the poor, the younger generation, and from God himself.

Thank God that he raises up some among us to meet the needs of the rock 'n roll generation. Thank God for David Wilkerson's willingness, years ago, to go to New York. Thank God for some of the recent youth work done by Youth for Christ workers. But much more is needed. And unless there is widespread repentance among the churches about our unthinking acceptance of every aspect of the free enterprise system, automation, and the virtue of high mechanical productivity, the alienation between us and those we seek to reach will increase.

Who is being worldly? We, the older generation, see rock festivals as harmful and urge Christian young people to stay away from them. Young people from our churches who go to them are considered worldly. But we are worldly, too. Their form of worldliness consists of accepting the values, goals, and lifestyle of their generation. Our worldliness consists of accepting the values, goals and lifestyle of ours. And until we examine and repent of the divorce between our spiritual professions and our material ambitions, or recognize that those externals which distinguish us from non-Christians are trivial, while those that identify us with our culture are far from trivial, we shall continue to be people trying to cast motes out of our children's eyes while our vision is obstructed by the logs in our own.

Questions for Study and Discussion

1. Is there any unchanging criterion by which we can judge the morality of musical sounds and rhythms?

2. To what degree should personal taste determine the music we listen to? What other factors are important?

3. In what sense are a song's words, or lyrics, more explicitly moral or immoral, spiritual or worldly, than its musical score?

4. Discuss the underlying reasons for the use and abuse of both illegal and prescription drugs among young people and adults. How do these reasons reflect worldliness?

5. What are some of the symptoms of a "production oriented" society? How might such trends be reversed?

6. "The externals which distinguish us from non-Christians are trivial, while those that identify us with our culture are far from trivial." Pinpoint the externals in both these categories.

6

THE WORLD
AND SEXUAL MORALITY

I DON'T REALLY KNOW HOW IT all came about. Doubtless the Devil was behind it—he's behind a lot of things—but it's all too easy to explain everything bad by blaming Satan and forget that we Christians had something to do with it too.

I once wrote a book called *Eros Defiled*. I wrote it because I was deeply troubled about the lack of help for Christians involved in sexual sin, believers who needed help not from a psychiatrist but from the church. I was so deeply troubled that I did something I did not know then that I could do. I wrote a book.

Two people's reactions puzzled me. The first comment came from an elder in the church I preached in around that time.

"John," he said, "You've got an exaggerated idea of the danger of sexual sin. You only think the way you do because you're a psychiatrist." (I may not be quoting him accurately, but certainly that was the gist of what he said.)

The other reaction came when I sent my manuscript to a well-known Christian publishing house. The substance of the letter they returned with my rejected manuscript can be summarized as follows: "This is not the kind of book Christians need; what they need is a book on how Christian couples can enjoy sex in the marital bed."

I suspect the publisher was politely lying (publishers and editors lie like the rest of us). I know that, because the editor of an outstanding Christian magazine returned an article I wrote many years ago, saying that it was rejected because my syntax and sentence structure were not all they should be. Naively, I wrote back begging him to tell me what was wrong with my sentence structure. I wanted to learn, and was horrified to think my English was as bad as he implied. Well, there was a pause of a few weeks. When the reply finally came the editor confessed that the real problem had nothing to do with syntax. My article was rejected because one member of the editorial committee had objected to my suspected softness on a premillenarian, pretribulation rapture. (God bless that honest editor! It took courage for him to write as he did.) So I sent my article to the old *Sunday School Times,* whose editors accepted and published it.

Sometimes I wonder whether the Christian publisher was lying about *Eros Defiled;* he had an editorial committee to counsel him, too. I thank God for InterVarsity Press, whose editors have always been absolutely straight with me.

Whatever the reasons, Christians have become more and more like the world in their sexual standards. *Eros Defiled* helped some people greatly, but it did little or nothing to stem the tide of Christians choosing the path of sexual gratification, even though it often involved sin.

Mental versus physical impurity

One of the younger editors of *Eros Defiled* commented that the chapter on premarital sex was the one that showed the least understanding and empathy with current attitudes and practice. He was probably right. I was a virgin when I married. I had never even messed around. I had never touched a woman. So, perhaps without realizing it, I was writing like a Pharisee. I had had fantasies—had I *ever* had fantasies! I dreamed, I lusted, I did things which I wouldn't want anyone to know about—not with actual women, or men, or animals or any living creature. But I was a lustful slave to eroticism. Only a merciful God could pardon the sexual distortions I indulged in mentally.

That is why I am in no position to look down on Christian youngsters who indulge in petting, or even in intercourse. The only reason I didn't fornicate was because I was too scared. My generation of young people just didn't dare. We were protected by concrete walls of fear and taboo. But we were not a whit more virtuous than the present fornicating generation. In our own way we were just as troubled, and just as guilty. Yet am I going to say that premarital sex is ever justifiable? Never! What I do say is that the younger generation is not receiving from the churches, any more than in my generation, the help they need to maintain God's standards of mental as well as physical purity.

The double standard: preaching vs. practice

One of my patients, a woman in her thirties, told me a year or so ago about the young people's group in the church she had attended as an adolescent. There was a look of amusement on her face as she replied to a question I asked. "*Of course* they taught us that premarital sex was wrong," she said, "but after the talks on sex we went outside and had a good laugh as we proceeded to break into couples and have sex. The talks didn't mean a thing."

What has happened to change the sexual mores in one generation? Why is promiscuity so much more common now than in my own youth? I and my peers were virgins because the strong taboos of the churches were shared, to a considerable degree, by society as a whole. We all knew what must *never* be done, even though we were never given adequate reasons why. We were occasionally warned against sexual sin because it led to pregnancy or venereal disease and we understood, intuitively, that nobody had anything but contempt for homosexuals. We avoided sexual sin because of our fears of unwanted parenthood, disease, and social rejection.

Today those taboos and fears have vanished. Birth control devices are easily available and birth control methods are taught in schools, which routinely supply the biological information about reproduction while studiously avoiding moral or value judgments which might infringe on personal freedom or belief. (True non-judgmentalism is, however, a logical impossibility. To forbid or exclude a value judgment is to assume, unconsciously, that the highest value is to have no values.) The sort of commitment to a lifetime relationship that Christian marriage demands is viewed as unreasonable, unnecessary, and even unhealthy. Homosexuality is presented as a viable alternative to heterosexuality. Literally, anything goes, except self-discipline, obedience to biblical principles, sexual abstinence before marriage, and faithfulness to one's marriage partner. Our young people are exposed to a society that countenances unparalleled promiscuity, and to churches so out of touch with the relevant Scriptures and so spiritually bankrupt that they are ripe for Satan's plucking.

Just two days ago, a Christian girl of twenty was telling me of her dilemma. She must choose between two boy friends. She has been going with one for four years, but she is getting bored with him. A more recent relationship is with a new convert to Christianity who was previously a wild boy around town. She intends to marry neither. With her steady boy friend she practices mutual masturbation to orgasm. She and her new flame have oral-genital sex to orgasm. It's a lot of fun, she says. She is typical of a large proportion of Christian young people today.

What lesson can we learn from such stories? We can learn, I suppose, that when preachers speak out against sexual sin, the preaching may achieve nothing, except calloused consciences in their hearers. Most evangelical Christian pastors, if they speak about sex at all, denounce premarital sex, extramarital sex, homosexuality, and divorce. In spite of this, the sexual behavior of Christians has reached the point of being indistinguishable from that of non-Christians. The divorce rate among alumni of one of North America's most prestigious Christian colleges is said to equal or exceed the national average. Unhappily, reliable studies on the subject are hard to come by. But the observable facts speak loud and clear—outstanding Christians—pastors, counsellors, and spiritual leaders, indulge in illicit relationships and/or get divorces and yet continue in their ministries and in leadership positions without penalty, almost without comment.

My information is based on the responses I receive to talks I give to old and young alike. I should make it clear that I dislike talking and writing about sex, and wish I could avoid such an emphasis. But who can hold his peace when sexual sin in the churches increases month by month? The one encouraging fact is that when I do speak, sexual sinners feel free to come to me after the meeting to confess their failures and to ask for help.

Divorce is almost becoming expected among Christians. It is both a painful and a controversial subject. It always has been. When Jesus was on earth, the famous Hillel-Shammi debate was raging. Rabbi Hillel (who would now be called a male-chauvinist pig) affirmed that men could divorce their wives for almost any reason, and Rabbi Shammi insisted that divorce was called for only when a woman was sexually unclean. Both spoke from the man's perspective, but Shammi more conservatively than Hillel.

Much has already been written about divorce. All I can do here is to share my own perspective on it, without trying to defend my limited understanding. It seems to me that Jesus had a purpose in juxtaposing his teaching on adultery and divorce. In all ages *some* divorces have been an excuse for what would otherwise be called adultery; we sometimes call it serial monogamy.

Jesus and divorce

Jesus taught that neither adultery nor divorce was in the plan of God. No adultery. No divorces (Matt. 19:18; 5:27-32). An exception was made (because of human sin and failure) where adultery was already destroying a marriage (Mark 10:4-9). To protect the woman in such circumstances, a special social status was acknowledged; given a bill of divorcement by her husband, she would become as a single woman once again, and be free to marry. Had there been no such provision the woman would have been condemned either to a life of loneliness and abuse or else what would have been tantamount to an adulterous marriage.

The thrust of Jesus' words is that many divorces were (and are) an excuse for legalized adultery. A man who desired an attractive woman was permitted, according to the views of Rabbi Hillel, to divorce his wife and marry the woman he lusted for. The same rationalization prevails today. Nor need the lusting begin as eroticism. As often as not, the way is paved for divorce when I, as either a man or a woman, discover how green the grass is on the other side of the fence—that is to say, how much more compatible and intelligent and understanding, how much kinder, and so on, is the partner I don't have than the one I do. The moment such a discovery is made, the door to adultery and divorce begins to open. Jesus condemned divorce and remarriage, correctly judging it to be based on sexual lust as well as desire for qualities other than sexual attractiveness.

The withering of a marriage

How often it happens—a marriage begins to go sour.

The symptoms include estrangement, tensions, family stresses, job conflicts, in-law problems, quarrels about money or sex or child-rearing. Then one or the other (or both) finds comfort in sharing their heartaches with a kind, understanding friend of the opposite sex.

Mary suddenly finds in her office manager, Bill, a totally different kind of man than her husband, Bob. Bill listens. He doesn't say too much but he is always willing to hear her problems and he tries to understand. He also defends Bob from time to time. "It must be rough on him, too, Mary. Maybe *he's* hurting."

The two have coffee together. One day they meet for lunch. Bill is looking troubled. Quite a way into their conversation Mary discovers the deep hurts in her office manager's marriage. "And all this time I've been unloading my troubles on you, Bill. Why didn't you tell me? I feel so ashamed—you holding your pain in and me pouring it out."

Eventually they have dinner together. They discuss together ways of making their marriages work. But you know already how the story ends; before long Mary is thinking, "If only I had a husband like Bill!" Bill is thinking, "If I had Mary as a wife...."

This "innocent" relationship is another aspect of that lusting after a woman in one's heart which Jesus condemned. It is a lust that leads just as directly to divorce and remarriage as does erotic lust. Whatever their faults may have been, neither Bill's wife nor Bob had been unfaithful. Perhaps even if they had, both marriages might have been saved and enriched.

But you see, once you have a psychological out, that is to say, once you perceive an attractive alternative to the trouble-ridden marriage you are now struggling with, it becomes just about impossible to work through the difficulties. The pull toward divorce and remarriage will tear you out of the arms of your spouse. You will become psychologically incapable of seeing how your present marriage can be worked out.

Three options for a troubled marriage

Marital conflicts may go one of three ways. First, they may lead to a chronically unsatisfactory arrangement where the partners can neither live together in harmony nor live apart. They end up living to make each other miserable, a habit which sometimes becomes too strong to break. How strange that it should be so—two people living together in order to hurt each other; two people in whom the lust to hurt has outgrown the yearning to love and be loved, yet both so needy that they are drawn together not by mere hostility but by the fear of abandonment or economic hardship; cruelty slowly refined in the marriage as each partner discovers and plays on the vulnerabilities of the other until both retire to lick their wounds before renewing the battle; wives who challenge their husbands by saying, "Hit me! Go on, hit me, you big bully! I won't stop you—*hit* me!", and husbands who respond as they are expected to; men who learn the role of martyrs, who walk around the house looking injured, performing small household chores with an air of piety and self-righteousness. The possibilities of such self-defeating relationships are endless, but the number of these marriages is decreasing and the partners in question are often middle-aged, or older.

The second option, separation or divorce, is now more

possible, more respectable, more economically feasible, and thus more common.

I have yet to encounter a problem-free marriage. The irony lies in the fact that the two alternatives mentioned —divorce or settled marital hostility—both entail pain. Separation or divorce are never easy options. For most people they are traumatic. I read about painless divorces in popular magazine articles, and I suppose they exist, but all I have seen (and they are many) have been unspeakably tragic.

Thus the third option is really the only biblical one— the stresses of a problem marriage may lead to a call for help or counsel, to the discovery of new insights and attitudes, and eventually to a firmer and stronger commitment to the marriage. Communication can become truer, more honest and more loving, less exaggerated and violent, gentler, freer, and the marriage can begin to grow again.

I cannot here discuss all the complex dynamics of marriage. In any case, the market is flooded with how-to-get-along-with-your-spouse books. All I can say is that the stresses that destroy marriages are as effective for *con*struction as they are for *des*truction.

There must, of course, be a willingness by both partners to do two things—each must be willing to see and acknowledge his or her own faults and weaknesses and each must also be able to accept the faults and acknowledge (and be grateful for) the strengths of the other. Marriage is always a risk. I cannot even predict the future course of my own marriage. Our first twenty-six years have been years of anger, tears, forgiveness, immaturity, love, and astonishing growth. We have learned to respect and trust each other's strengths and abilities (fortunately, they complement each other). We have also learned a certain amount of honesty about our weaknesses and have learned to laugh about them, with genuine amusement and less defensiveness. We have decided, quite illogically, that we deserve each other, yet that God has, in putting us together, given each of us far more than we deserve. And while we cannot predict the future, we no longer fear it.

From our own lives, then, we can say that God's "no divorce" rule is not harsh, but merciful, in that it has forced us to examine and resolve conflicts and enter a stronger, richer stage of marriage. At the same time, we know that the same mercy can be shown by God to those who have known both divorce and remarriage.

Meanwhile, the world looks on. Do we Christians have any real distinctives? Our sexual standards may be of the highest, but in our behavior and in the way we face our problems there is little to distinguish us from non-Christians. God has called us to lives of holiness. Jesus prayed that we might be left in the world but be delivered from the Evil One. But in our sexual behavior we, as a Christian community, are both in the world, and of it.

Questions for Study and Discussion

1. Contrast the sexual virtue of earlier generations with that of young people today. In what ways was the earlier generation as guilty and troubled as are today's young people?

2. Define true virginity. Why is virginity before marriage a part of God's good plan for human beings?

3. How do the sexual mores of a worldly society affect Christian standards of personal purity?

4. Discuss how churches are failing to help young people today in the area of sexual standards and practices. Why does the denunciation of immorality from church platforms today achieve so little?

5. Summarize Jesus' teaching on adultery and divorce.

6. What desires other than sexual ones may lead to divorce and remarriage?

7. Discuss the three options for a troubled marriage as described by the author. Which are the easiest options? The most satisfactory? Why is Jesus' strict "no divorce" rule the most merciful in the long run?

7

THE WORLD AND THE HOMOSEXUAL

Forty years ago few people would have thought of justifying homosexual practices. Most of my schoolmates snickered and joked about the topic. We had accumulated a store of inaccurate lore about male homosexuals (we had neither interest in nor understanding of female homosexuality)—information about "queers," "fairies," "dirty old men," and effeminate young men. Homosexuals were objects of ridicule and we enjoyed regaling one another with stories about their way of life and behavior. The stories were not erotic. Our amusement had to do with stereotypes of effeminacy which we could all mimic to our own entire satisfaction. Homosexuals lisped. They were sissies. They had a preference for green suits and brown hats (though none of us had actually seen an effeminate, green-suited, brown-hatted, lisping male). I am now convinced that our mockery and mimicry concealed a deep fear that one day we might ourselves turn out to be homosexuals. By our humor we were reassuring ourselves.

Curiously, most of us indulged (the sexes were separated in British schools) in the game of who was the quickest and most successful in making a grab for another boy's crotch as we passed one another in the halls between classes. The play was not exactly erotic. You guarded your own genitals but felt you had scored if you grabbed someone else's. It was a sort of masculine one-upmanship; nevertheless it opened the way to homosexual arousal.

During those same years in British public schools (the British term for exclusive, expensive, private schools) homosexuality, in the form of pederasty, was widespread. C. S. Lewis clearly describes the situation at Malvern School in his book *Surprised by Joy,* a situation that was by no means unique. And homosexual practices in the older British universities have been sensationally linked with a series of well-publicized spy scandals in the postwar period.

But the corruption of the effete members of the British upper class seemed, at the time, to be quite remote from the evangelical scene. It was true that occasional scandals arose involving child-molesting scout masters and minor Christian youth leaders. But such incidents were discussed in shocked whispers behind closed doors. There was no question in anyone's mind as to whether such activities were an option for Christians. Who could have foreseen in those days the open and widespread practice of homosexuality among both men and women, which now flourishes throughout the Western world, including both hemispheres of the Americas. (I have no statistics, but six years ago as I journeyed through Latin America and talked with Latin students, gay practices among Latin males seemed to be eroding the universal machismo.)

The growing public acceptance of homosexuality was revealed a couple of years ago by *Time* magazine in an article featuring homosexual communities. It described an area in a major U.S. city where citizen bands and human rights groups patrolled the gay area in order to protect gay citizens from vengeful gangs of young hoodlums. While it cannot by any means be said that gays have won complete acceptance in U.S. society, the Gay Rights movement has made big strides against discrimination and won a degree of acceptance that would have been unthinkable years ago.

Two extremes

A few years ago Anita Bryant, a courageous singer who may have been tragically naive about the ruthless politics surrounding the issue, typified the thrust of what is now known as the Moral Majority, which favors stringent measures against homosexuals, particularly opposing their employment in schools and government offices, and sees homosexuality as a dangerously corrupting influence which has the potential of destroying the West.

At the other extreme, a number of church groups—Roman Catholic, liberal protestant, and evangelical—are taking a very different stand. Their views can be summarized as follows: homosexuality is a natural condition and is in no way the fault of the homosexual person. A homosexual relationship may be regarded as God's gracious gift to the homosexual. To avoid promiscuity and demoralization among homosexuals, the church must welcome them, should encourage faithful relationships among them (giving public blessing to homosexual marriages), and should promote gatherings where the social needs of homosexuals can be met. It is even recommended that homosexuals be allowed to adopt children. I have talked to faculty members of an evangelical liberal arts school who assured me that professedly Christian counselors have counselled some of their students to accept God's gift of their sexual orientation and to act according to their "true" natures. (My friend Ken Blue, of Vancouver, recently came across a church where homosexuals were warned against the "sin" of having relations with someone of the opposite sex, the presumption being that if one were a homosexual, one should be true to one's nature!)

An important distinction

Is the practice of homosexuality wrong? Notice, please, that it is to *the practice* I point, not to the condition. The fact that some of us are attracted to our own sex represents temptation, not sin. As temptation, it differs in no way from other forms of sexual temptation. The distinction between *the practice* of homosexuality and *the orientation* of attraction to one's own sex is important. If, by homosexuals, we mean persons attracted to their own sex, then we will have to say that homosexuality is *not* sinful. It represents temptation, not sin. But according to the Bible the practice of homosexuality is sinful. Many Christian men and women, not understanding this distinction, carry around with them the secret shame and pain of a temptation they have never given way to—or if they have, only in a brief, regretted moment of weakness.

"The Bible says nothing specifically about the homosexual condition (despite the rather misleading RSV translation of 1 Cor. 6:9), but its condemnations of homosexual behaviour are explicit. The scope of these strictures must, however, be carefully determined. Too often they have been used as tools of a homophobic polemic which has claimed too much" (D. H. Field, in *The Illustrated Bible Dictionary,* 3 vols., [Tyndale House, 1980], 2:657). How *does* the Scripture view homosexuality? In the Old Testament the strictures arise out of the association of homosexual prostitution with idolatrous cults. It is condemned (Lev. 18:22; 20:13) because this sort of worship was common both in surrounding pagan nations and in those peoples the Israelites had conquered. God called this kind of worship "an abomination." The force of condemnation of homosexuality in Leviticus has to do with this association. The worship of Yahweh was to be kept free from idolatrous prostitution, male or female. But the practices were not easily shaken off. In the early days of Judah's history we read, "There were even male shrine prostitutes in the land; the people engaged in all the detestable practices of the nations whom the Lord had driven out before the Israelites (1 Kings 14:24 NIV; see also 1 Kings 15:12; 22:46). These passages describe homosexual practices indulged in by men with the aid of skillfully trained homosexual prostitutes.

Homosexuality today has no connection with idolatrous cults, but is hedonistic. Does that make it acceptable? Paul's strongly worded passage in Romans 1:24-27 makes it clear that homosexual acts are sinful acts. They are included in the dismal catalogue of "wickedness, evil, greed and depravity. . . . envy, murder, strife, deceit and malice. They (those who reject God) are gossips, slanderers . . ." (Rom. 1:29-30 NIV).

Yet while Paul makes it clear that the list of evils is offensive to a holy God, that is not exactly the point he is making in Romans 1. Rather he is describing the horrible curse that came upon headstrong men and women who refused to acknowledge their Creator but arrogantly made gods of their own.

The result? "Since they did not think it worthwhile to retain the knowledge of God, *he gave them over to a depraved mind,* to do what ought not to be done."

Homosexual tendencies are thus described as part of the curse of our fallen condition, and our stubborn insistence on making gods of our own. Along that way always lies sin, ruin, and the curse. Paul's argument is not an explicit attempt to condemn the sin of homosexuality but to show how mankind opened human society to a host of evil practices (including homosexuality) which destroy human relations, and therefore human society, from within.

Homosexual tendencies are *not* a beautiful gift from God. They are part of the curse God permitted to fall upon men and women and upon the very ground from which we all gained our sustenance. The curse has become ever more deeply imbedded among and around us as we have continued to shut God out.

From the beginning it was not so. At the dawn of creation the human being was divided into a complementary pair—a male and a female, unashamed in their nakedness. They were formed for mutual comfort and companionship, and to provide that context of love in which children should ideally be conceived, born, and reared.

But the fall touched every part of our nature. Homosexual tendencies, like tendencies to lie, to steal, to hate, to exploit one another, are all the outcome of the Fall. When the shame of nakedness arose, all sexual relations were affected.

Let us be clear then that homosexual acts are sinful acts and need to be repented of, and that a homosexual lifestyle is a lifestyle displeasing to God. But it is also a lifestyle that is very difficult to quit, a lifestyle that calls for firm but loving rescue operations from God's people, not to the gathering of our Pharisee skirts about us in withdrawal from those whom our Savior came to deliver.

Ironically, homosexuality, once the Great Unmentionable, is now the Great Discussable, while lonely men and women with homosexual tendencies, or who have practiced homosexuality and wish to abandon it, do not dare to disclose their hearts and feelings to brothers and sisters in the average church. It is my hope that the situation will change, but what quiet checking I have done among the churches both in Winnipeg, and elsewhere in North America, leads me to a conservative guess that about one person in a hundred in the average evangelical church is either a practicing homosexual or a hurt and lonely homosexual struggler who may or may not have someone to share his or her burden with. Among the practicing homosexuals are both married and single men and women.

Is homosexuality worldly?

But where does homosexuality fit into a book on world-liness? Let us return to the idea that worldliness may be viewed as similarity to the world, or as taking on the world's color to such an extent that Christians become indistinguishable from the world in their attitudes and practices, ceasing to be salt and light. We can see at once that if we apply this criterion to Christians who are prac-ticing homosexuals, or if we view the church as a body among whom the number of practicing homosexuals is constantly growing, then we must plead guilty to growing worldliness, since in this respect we are becoming in-creasingly like the world.

But the matter needs to be examined more carefully. It seems that the church mirrors the world in a deeper sense than the one I just mentioned. Non-Christians may be divided into three broad groups—those who express scorn, contempt, and hostility towards homosexuality; those who are bored by or indifferent to the subject; and those who champion the rights of homosexuals to live their lives according to their sexual orientation. And as I view the Christian scene I find the same three groups of people, the hostile and contemptuous, the bored and the ignorant, and the church's soft underbelly, the sentimen-tal organizers of support for the gay lifestyle. What I find strangely lacking are churches where the issue is faced and dealt with in a merciful but godly manner. *It is this lack that reflects the church's worldliness.* And, in turn, it is part of a wider problem. Evangelical churches are so structured that the mutual admonitions, mutual up-building, gentle reproving, and the firm discipline so commonly urged in the New Testament are difficult to implement for logistical reasons. How can we be intimately related with 3,000 church members? Howard Snyder in his books (*The Problem of Wineskins, The Community of the King,* and *The Radical Wesley*) deals with such issues. Many Christians whose hearts reach out for something more real and vital begin to meet in house fellowships, sometimes retaining their connection with the parent church, but at other times cutting themselves off. In his book, *Dynamics of Spiritual Life,* Richard Lovelace discusses the problem from a church historian's perspective and sees as critical the relationship between what he calls the *micro-* and the *macro-*communities of the church. The fact is that churches do not provide the kind of climate in which members may share and request help for their problems, nor does a degree of spiritual intimacy exist which would make hidden sin difficult to conceal.

Church communities are thus worldly communities that, in the matter of homosexuality, reflect society as a whole. But they need not continue to be so. Change is painful and difficult but there are signs that it may be on the way.

How can the church help?

One large church I know, where provision is made for intimate fellowship as well as the joys of the meeting together in a large congregation, has a story that moved me greatly when I heard it. An elder of the church who had been a practicing homosexual before his conversion some years before, began to lapse into his former habits. The ministerial board eventually spent many hours counseling and praying with this brother, who seemed anxious for help, but word reached the ministers that the former elder was continuing to corrupt younger men. They made it clear to him at that point that the matter would have to be brought before the whole congregation.

In his shame and rage the brother left the church, defiantly and publicly continuing to lead a life of perversity and bitterly condemning the congregation that had so rejected him.

Seven years passed. One day a long letter came from the man in question, addressed to the ministers, to be read to the congregation. In the letter he acknowledged how wrong he had been, admitting his deceit, his subsequent actions, and his bitter attitude and words. He asked for forgiveness, having repented and turned from his sin, and he confessed hope that somehow he might find a place in the Christian community once more.

The ministerial board lost no time in getting in touch with him and, satisfied with the genuineness of his repentance, told the congregation what had happened. What provoked my tears of joy was the manner in which they received him back. The congregation arranged a barbecue meal at which they roasted a calf, and after which they gave him a leather jacket and put a new gold ring on his finger.

I cry to God that he will change worldly evangelical churches and teach us what redemptive love and godly discipline can do to make us shine in the darkness of the world around. Let us devote our attention less to opposing the appointment of practicing lesbians to the ministry. Let us rather think with compassion about all homosexuals, and particularly about Christians who have fallen into homosexual practices. The difficulties of abandoning the lifestyle are far greater than most of us realize. A homosexual is accepted by the homosexual community. He or she would not be welcomed in most churches, nor find help in being delivered from a homosexual lifestyle. In one major Californian city lesbians promote lesbianism aggressively, seducing young girls (including Christian girls) and having seduced them, tell them, "You are one of us now. The straight community will never accept you back," and there is only too much truth in what they say.

Meanwhile our churches, like secular associations, are concerned with fund-raising, beautiful buildings, large numbers, comforting sermons from highly qualified preachers, while they display indifference to the poor, and to the pariahs of society—drunks, whores, homosexuals, the poor, the insane, and the lonely. Jesus himself would find no place in our all-too-respectable churches, for he did not come to help the righteous but to bring sinners to repentance. Our churches are not equipped to do that sort of thing. We fail constantly to exhort members. As for discipline, even the grave sins of pride, untruthfulness, and lack of love go uncorrected.

May God have mercy on us all! In a day to come Christ will not only express his wrath against those who choose a homosexual lifestyle, but also against those of us who failed in the hour of their need to minister loving, healing discipline to the homosexuals among us.

Questions for Study and Discussion

1. Contrast the attitudes of the Moral Majority and religious liberal groups to the gay rights movement. Where do you fit, in the broad spectrum of opinion regarding homosexuals?

2. Briefly describe your personal experience of, or contact with, homosexual individuals.

3. At what point, in the author's opinion, does homosexuality become sinful?

4. Referring to such passages as Leviticus 18:22; 20:13; 1 Kings 14:24; 15:12; 22:46 and Romans 1:24, summarize the Bible's view of homosexual practices.

5. What is the biblical evidence that homosexuality was not part of God's original pattern for human beings?

6. What makes homosexuality worldly?

7. What three worldly attitudes toward gays are found in the church? What fourth attitude does the author think is needed for the church to come to grips with the problem?

8

DOING AS THE ROMANS DO

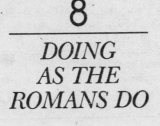

PERHAPS THERE IS NO POINT at which we are more similar to the world than in our patriotism, in our sense of national pride. I first began to reflect about this one July Fourth, when I was privileged to be present in a school for missionaries' children in Bolivia. Most of the children and staff were U.S. citizens.

I was British. My wife, Lorrie, was Canadian. At first we were happy to see the fun and the rejoicing of children and staff. I had never felt that the United States should have remained a part of Britain and believed that the attitude of the British government at the time of the American Revolution was both stupid and shortsighted. So I had no bad feelings about being a representative of the former "enemy." In any case, time has long since calmed the feelings that once ran so high. Yet, as the day wore on, both Lorrie and I felt increasingly uneasy and uncomfortable. Since our first years on the mission field, we had come to realize how little nationality mattered. Since we were all citizens of heaven, we felt that our earthly citizenship was of academic interest only.

But on that particular Fourth of July we suddenly found we were outsiders. I'm sure no one intended to hurt us, for our fellow missionaries were all warm-hearted and loving. But they shared something we didn't share, something that went beyond loyalty to the United States and was more like old-fashioned patriotism and national-istic fervor about being American. For the first time we were truly outsiders looking in. Were we being too sensitive? Perhaps so. But it hurt. Rather childishly and very rudely I refused to stand when the U.S. national anthem was sung. At that point I was more to be blamed than any of my American brothers and sisters who were simply enjoying their national celebration. I, on the other hand, was being bitter.

But long after I let the Lord deal with my childish bitterness I continued to reflect on the meaning of issues like patriotism, loyalty, and pride in one's earthly coun-try. For the first time I could feel from inside my heart and understand some of the hurt that Latin Americans experience from some Western missionaries.

Patriotism vs. true loyalty

Let me try to define my terms, not perhaps as the dic-tionary does, but according to the nuances that common usage has given them. Christians, I believe, should always be loyal to the countries of which they are citizens. But patriotism is another matter. Patriotism means sticking up for your side, being proud to belong to it, perhaps even a little boastful about it no matter what the circumstances. Patriotism says, "My country—may she always be right—but my country, right or wrong." Christians who are patriotic in this sense are not merely in the world. They are *of* it.

Loyalty is different. My truest loyalty will forthrightly oppose that which is wrong in my country (and I am either a fool or a jingoist if I pretend my country is the most virtuous under the sun). Loyalty refuses either to abandon its country in its difficulties or to tolerate its sins and weaknesses. To my mind, Jeremiah is the supreme example of loyalty to Judah and to the city of Jerusalem. He never once deserted his country. He stuck around long after his exhortations had made him *persona non grata*. Yet he never ceased to oppose its wrong-doing. And in some strange way he won the respect of his fellow countrymen, who dragged him with them down to Egypt, protesting to the last.

What children are taught in schools is patriotism, not loyalty. It was patriotism that led some Brethren Assemblies to back Hitler's Nazi regime; it was loyalty that led other Plymouth Brethren Assemblies to stand against it. (And it was the grace of God that restored harmony between the two groups when the war was over, and allowed the bitterness to die away.) Bonhoeffer was not patriotic. But he thought and prayed and spoke and wrote out of the deep loyalty for which he died in the end.

In their excellent review of civic religion, *Twilight of*

97

the Saints, Linder and Pierard have described how the U.S. government made use of religious sentiment in fomenting patriotism among the citizenry of the United States. Such patriotism was shortsighted, superficial, artificial, and in the ultimate sense carnal. True loyalty is faithful and responsible, and in that sense spiritual.

Ultimately, each of us will have to choose between loyalty (loyalty to Christ and to our duty as citizens to seek the best for our country) and patriotism (the naive assumption that our country is basically sound and that all we need is another change of government). Patriotic people may form new political parties—even "evangelical" ones. Patriotic people will always seek power in the object of their patriotism, where loyal citizens may, in the end, be sent to jail and shot. If you think I am joking, read church history. Upon whom did the wrath of Roman citizens fall when Nero needed scapegoats? What happens to Christians who meet in secret in Russia today? They are hard-working, productive, upright, and responsible. They love Christ and Russia. They are tortured and executed while the communist bureaucrats, in love with power and willing to echo party slogans, are rewarded with political position and prestige. What has happened repeatedly in the past will happen again in the future. The loyalty of true Christians becomes suspect in times of national crisis because they are honest, even outspoken, about their nation's shortcomings. So, if one is loyal, one may be in the world but not of it. But to be patriotic is to be of the world.

Dressing as the Romans dress

What should Christians wear? Ask that question and you

will get almost as many answers to that as there are Christians. Most of us have already made up our minds about how we want to dress and rationalize the style we have already chosen in terms of the image we have decided to project.

Should Christians be distinctive in their dress? Well there's a new Christian women's fashion magazine that gives us hints on how to be both smart and sanctified. Tweeds, we gather, are the "in" Christian thing, appropriate for worship in the winter. Accessories add to the look of Christian chic.

I believe everything we do reflects our inner values and attitudes. Therefore our dress will inevitably reflect what we are. Perhaps this should be our starting point. Too often when we try to "dress Christian" we begin with the dress and try to adjust our inner attitudes to fit the outer appearance, which is, of course, what man sees. And thus we elevate man's opinion above God's, who looks at hearts.

This problem, I am sure, was at the origin of the habits of monks and nuns, or the distinctive clothing of groups like the Amish, the Hutterites, some Mennonites, and Salvationists. Yet all of us are affected in one way or another. After a while we can generally pick out the religious group someone belongs to by clothing style, even when it is not a uniform. For dress is important to us. Most of us feel good when we are dressed well, and ill at ease when we are not. Our tastes may differ widely. For some, good dress means faded jeans. Sporty or svelte, "preppy" or "peasant-look," we have our varied preferences. But the principle remains the same. We feel good when we are dressed like those whom we admire most.

So how should a Christian dress? "Together" Christians are all for proving, once and for all, that Christians are *not* dowdy and unattractive. Wigs and false eyelashes and four-inch heels are *in* according to some women, who rationalize their styles by saying, "I gotta be me."

Psychologists tell us that dress is also a form of sexual attraction. This may be only one aspect of the matter, and it may be more obvious in female than male fashions. But men are catching on. Notice the tight crotches of the men's pants in the Sears catalogs. Notice the deep hairy necklines in men's shirts, with their heavy gold chains or pendants. Notice, too, the emphasis on the tan, symbol of the hedonistic sun-worshiper. Surely Christians ought to be as sexy and suntanned as the world is! After all, God made both sex and sun! It is easy to rationalize almost anything our little hearts desire. The Christian community is so multi-faceted and varicolored that we're bound to fit in with *someone*.

For better or worse, and whether we are conscious of it or not, it is true that dress is part of our sexuality. However, it will quickly lose what outrageous or blatantly sexual connotations it has if it remains always the same. Fashions must therefore change. But if fashion houses didn't do it for us (in order to render last year's fashions outmoded, and make more money on this year's), some of us would start doing it ourselves.

It is the *new* and bizarre that is sexually provocative. Two-piece bathing suits got to be pretty boring after a while even when they shrank to briefer and briefer dimensions, so that new one-piece lines had to be invented to emphasize different body areas and shapes.

And what is true of swimwear is true of all types of clothing.

So what about sexual attraction and the Christian? You have to admit that Peter had a point: a woman's deepest form of sexual attraction is her inner tranquility. Nothing attracts a man like that. (Unfortunately Peter forgot to tell us what is at the core of male attractiveness.) He advised wives, "Your beauty should not come from outward adornment, it should be that of your inner self, the unfading beauty of a gentle and quiet spirit which is of real worth in God's sight" (1 Pet. 3:3-4). His point was not that women should not braid and bejewel their hair (or whatever they did with it in those days), but that all the hair arranging in the world is no substitute for inner tranquility. There is so much more to sexual attraction than eroticism. And, needless to say, there is more to dress than sexuality. Convenience, comfort, and protection, for example.

Let me get back, then, to our inner attitudes and how they should be reflected in our dress. As our walk with God gets closer and more constant, our sexual as well as our general insecurity should diminish. For that reason, our need to be in the avant-garde of fashion will also diminish. Again, the way we spend our money will change. We will probably be more content to buy last season's fashions at sale prices.

You may ask me for some rules and guidelines, but I refuse to legislate about the matter, since legislation is the high road to legalism. I suspect that happy and well-adjusted Christians, while neat and attractive, will be less concerned about and spend less time and money on clothing than other people, and will tend to be a little behind rather than ahead of the latest fashions. Whether women wear jewelry, make-up, have pierced ears or fake eyelashes, or whether men splash themselves with Musk, dangle gold chains round their necks, and wear Gucci shoes—these are not the basic issues. What is significant is my peace of heart, my certainty that a gracious, loving God cares for me, and that dress is not the most important thing in the world. If I am a little disorganized and don't always know how to match my colors, my clothing will reflect that, too. But so what? People are not alienated from Christ just because my socks don't match my suit or my tie is badly tied. Dowdiness is not the great spiritual tragedy that some people make it out to be. It will not take somebody long to discover the inner me, the me that is not too worried about clothes, but who likes people and loves Jesus.

Do we seriously believe that Jesus needs high fashion to bring human beings to himself? All that haute couture will do is to draw the fashion conscious to *us,* so that like so many Christian peacocks we may display our plumage and strut around, admiring one another and assuring one another of the powerful witness of our spiffy outfits. And our mutually admiring circle will be *of* the world as well as *in* it.

But if we are like Jesus there will be an inner peace that influences the way our muscles move. There is a joy at the core of us that is reflected in our eyes and the tones of our voices and the way we respond in conversation. There is a real humility inside, an unselfconsciousness which makes us relatively indifferent to the impression we make by our external appearance.

As for our uniforms, whether they are of some Catholic religious order or some Protestant distinctive, all they do is make most people say, "If *that's* what you have to do to be a truly sanctified Christian, then forget it!"

Christian retirement

How do Christians differ from non-Christians in retirement? Hardly at all. They set up their retirement funds and when they retire, they spend at least their winters and sometimes their whole year in Florida, or California, or Arizona. I speak, of course, of those whose financial resources permit such a life. But I suspect many more of us would do the same if we only had the money, and dream about it even though we don't.

What is retirement? A time to take it easy? A time for travel to exotic lands? A time to devote oneself to one's hobbies? A time for daily golf with congenial friends? A time to enjoy the grandchildren when they come for a couple of weeks in the sun (and a time to breathe a sigh of relief when their visit is over)? Everything depends on one's major focus in life.

I know what I hope to do when I retire. I want to study. I want to have more time to pray and preach. I want to write. Obviously my wants may not be the same as yours. But what I am trying to say is that I do not, must not, and God helping me, *will* not retire from the conflict with the powers of darkness. For me to live is Christ, and I look forward intensely to additional time for the great battle—my Lord's battle—and the opportunity to take part in it.

How, then, may we test for worldliness? How important is God's work to you now? What are your retirement plans? There are two tests you can apply. Are you doing things for God *now* or are you postponing them till you retire? If you are postponing them now, you will most likely postpone them till you die.

A second test concerns what you envision for yourself when you retire. Florida? Arizona? Hawaii? The good life? Freedom from rheumatism ("I feel so much better when I'm down there")? I dread Manitoba winters—they are so long and so bitterly cold, and I have an awful feeling God may want me to stay right here. Yet I know that if Manitoba is where he wants me and can use me, then I would rather choose Jesus and snow, than Florida sunshine without his approval.

Entertainment evangelism

Christians behave as the world does in other crucial areas of life. Take the matter of evangelism. The issue is a difficult one because the Christian message should be presented in terms that are relevant to the culture in which it is presented. But such a principle may be carried too far. Every Christian enterprise needs a model, and the basic model we have adopted is the entertainment model. Most Christian TV shows, whatever positive comments we may make about them, are half hucksterism, half showmanship. From a technical viewpoint the showmanship is often superb. It rivets our attention. People turn their sets on, watch, and listen. Several Christian TV shows attract bigger audiences than do comparable commercial shows.

But what kind of Christianity does the entertainment model reflect and produce? It reflects a subculture with its own external image and jargon. In turn, it produces disciples of TV shows, needing their daily dose of entertainment. A more important question is: How does TV evangelism differ from the entertainment world in general? True, the ideational content differs. The shows are more family-oriented, but the ideational content may be relatively unimportant. It is the *model* that will leave the most indelible imprint, and the model is the world's model. In our evangelism—at the heart of the very reason the church is left here (to bear witness to Jesus) —we are not only in the world but *of* it.

We attract people to Jesus by entertaining them. We ignore the truth that *Jesus is not a pill needing a sugar coat.* He needs only to be lifted up, to be manifested. Do you retort that in TV evangelism he *is* being lifted up? In words perhaps, yes. But McLuhan is right. The medium is the message. And the medium is show-biz, superbly crafted and presented, but show-biz, nonetheless. So Christianity is increasingly seen as (and despised by thinking people for so being) a specialized form of show-biz.

But TV show-biz represents only the end product of a long process, a process that has arisen out of a star-spangled culture that includes the exploitation of Christian football heroes and Christian movie stars. Why do so many professional athletic teams tell Jesus they're trusting him for a win? Does the glory of Christ depend on a victory in a sports stadium? The cutting edge of our evangelism consists all too often of gimmickry and publicity stunts (and bumper stickers such as "I found it!" and "Honk if you love Jesus!").

Even in our missionary conventions we like to feature missionary heroes and pioneers, or, better still, "nationals" in all the glory of their colorful native dress.

Though I have no wish to criticize the many singers and musicians who seek to glorify God in their public praises, I find it a little more difficult to accept Christian chalk artists, magicians, and bell-ringers. Can you imagine Jesus training the disciples in conjuring tricks, acrobatics, or playing the musical saw? Or how about featuring Peter, James, and John as a men's trio?

True, Jesus and his followers belonged to a different culture. Their music, their dancing, their drama were different from ours. But there was entertainment in their world, too. Salome's dancing was a part of a tradition of dancing. What kinds of crowds might Jesus have attracted by regular public performances of traditional Jewish dances by Martha and Mary? Scholars may protest and say that such presentations would have been socially unacceptable at that time. But did Jesus ever worry about shattering nonessential social conventions?

The source of power

My point is that the cutting edge of Jesus' ministry was its undiluted truth and power. It was also the cutting edge of Paul's ministry, and of John Wesley's ministry. "Give me a hundred men who fear nothing but God and sin and I will turn England upside down!" Wesley cried. God gave him a hundred, and more, and England *was* turned upside down.

Howard Snyder begins his recent book, *The Radical Wesley,* as follows:

"It is early Sunday morning, May 30, 1742. The northern port city of Newcastle-upon-Tyne is hardly awake. Two strangers from London, one a slight man in his late thirties, walk quietly down Sandgate Street in 'the poorest and most contemptible part of the town.'

"The two men stop at the end of the street and begin singing the Hundredth Psalm. A few curious people gather and the shorter man starts preaching from Isaiah 53. . . . The knot of listeners grows to a crowd of several hundred, then over a thousand. When the small man stops, the crowd gapes in astonishment. So the preacher announces: 'If you desire to know who I am, my name is John Wesley. At five in the evening, with God's help, I design to preach here again.'

"That night Wesley finds a crowd of some 20,000 waiting. After he preaches, many urge him to stay longer. . . ."

Do you contend that such a phenomenon was due to the special circumstances of Wesley's day? That Wesley had no media outlets and knew nothing of advertising techniques, so that God had to do something special? Poor God! What a difficult time he must have had down the centuries, how limited he must have felt, before we were able to assist him with our modern technology! Just imagine what Jesus could have done with video tape!

Do we then blame Billy Sunday for his antics? Though not criticizing Moody and Sankey, or Torrey and Alexander and their sanctified showmanship, have we ever paused to reflect that in progressively adopting the entertainment model in our evangelism and even in our "worship," we may have chosen the second best and moved another step in the direction of being not only in the world but of it?

The Christian performing artist, like the preacher, faces formidable problems. It is incredibly difficult to sing or play solely to the glory of God with humility, after being brought on stage to applause, and praised to the skies by an emcee.

Let us stand back and view the whole process by which we set up our evangelistic and healing campaigns. How does the organization differ from the way cabaret is organized? Can we distinguish it from a political campaign?

Well, it is to be hoped there is the matter of prayer. Yet do we not, even in our praying, automatically limit God to the model we have already selected, and the plans already projected and budgeted for? How can God do a "new thing" in our midst when we insist that he do it only in ways we are culturally conditioned to understand and conform to?

So Christian conventions, political conventions, sales conventions, evangelistic campaigns, and cabaret shows all have features in common. And, once again, the medium has become the message.

In some ways I wish we would multiply our forces and do the thing properly. I wish good Christian dramatists would write for commercial radio and television programs and thus serve as leaven in the entertainment business. We need Christian novelists writing real novels for secular presses, real Christian playwrights who will write for Broadway. We also need more *small* evangelists, and *small* bands of Christians who are concerned with the neighbors they meet face to face every day in their own localities. We need small Bible study groups and lesser Bible teachers whose outreach is no impersonal expensive media show, but a sharing of Christ over coffee in the livingroom. It is that kind of personal, practical outreach in homes and house churches that has the power to turn whole cities upside down as the Word of God spreads from home to home across the city. But as matters stand, we are of the world as well as in it in that very, very vital matter—the proclamation of the evangel.

Glory-giving and getting. Another question: Does God really get the glory from our evangelism? I do not believe so. You disagree? Think for a minute. How do the media report our campaigns? To whom do *they* attribute our success? To *us,* of course. We may say we give God all the glory, but the world explains the whole thing by pointing to our organizational ability, to our publicity, to our revolutionary technology, to our performing artists, our preachers and our big names.

But when Jesus was on earth, there were men who gave glory to God as a result of his ministry. As Jesus walked along the Sea of Galilee healing the lame, the blind, the dumb, "the people were amazed . . . and they praised the God of Israel." (Matt. 15:13 NIV). Do today's non-Christians react spontaneously in this way? Very rarely. Even when we tell them to give glory to God they respond by admiring us for our spirituality and humility.

When Jesus healed the paralytic, the crowd was filled, not with excitement but with "awe; and they praised God who had given such power to men." I will recognize that the Holy Spirit is doing what he wants to do when newspaper editors throw their hands in the air and say "Something is going on here that no one can explain," or when newscasters shake their heads in amazement as they read the news and admit, "Mebbe there *is* a God after all. How else can you explain what's going on!" That I have yet to see, and as long as our evangelism is "of the world," I never will.

Going for the top

There is another attitude that demonstrates how thoroughly we are of the world as well as in it; it is our tendency to "go for the top." I have no objection to presidential breakfasts or to the evangelization of university students, for whom Christ certainly died. For that matter, I spent many years of my life involved with university evangelism. *But I did not do so because I want to "win tomorrow's leaders for Christ."* That represents politics, not evangelism. I preached to students because I belonged to the university world, and because I was burdened to witness to the world of which I was a part.

But we have politicized evangelism. We go for the important people, the men and women of influence. Why? Because our outlook is carnal.

Whom did Jesus seek to reach? Pilate? Members of the Sanhedrin? The Sadducees? The Roman government? Understand, I am not criticizing the thing itself. Politicians and university professors and brilliant students need to be converted like anybody else. Paul also preached on Mars Hill. Let us by all means attempt to reach all men. But the main thrust of the evangelism that has mattered down the ages has been *the evangelism among the poor.* Jesus spent his time principally among what we would now call "the disadvantaged."

He might accept the odd invitation to a Pharisee's house for a meal (but even then, there were embarrassing moments). But he lived, taught, walked, worked miracles among, fed, and blessed the poor.

I am myself ashamed that I do not do so, or that I do so very rarely. I don't know how to talk to the poor. I try to, but I don't do it very well. Occasionally, to my very great embarrassment, I find myself weeping when I try to explain the gospel—weeping because the gospel is so moving. But I'm not sure whether my listeners understand what I'm crying about.

And from whence do my speaking invitations come? From the rich. Always from big churches, the national organizations. What should I do? Accept? Reject? I am bewildered. And of course, one of the first questions many of them ask me is *what is my fee?* I don't know any more. Is anyone preaching to the poor?

Oh, I know there are city missions run by professionals and backed by respectable boards. Mostly they serve free meals to the drunks and bums who get saved twice a month. But the North American Indians, the blacks, the Cubans, the Portuguese, the boat people, the immigrants of a hundred nationalities struggling to survive among people of a strange tongue which they cannot understand, the women who work in clothing factories for sweat shops for a minimum wage—who preaches to them?

Meanwhile we go on reaching for the top—or at least for the middle class. Our evangelistic crusades have reserved seats for VIPs. Nice people make nice converts.

I do not exaggerate. I am weeping as I write. I don't know what to do. I am at a loss as to know how it can all be changed. Where is the God of Elijah? Where is the God of our Lord Jesus Christ?

Yet I have seen what God can do among the poorest of the poor. I have seen the Holy Spirit at work in the slums of Latin America. I do not only weep for sorrow (I am still weeping, but also for joy). I weep for joy at my friendship with new Christians in a Brazilian hovel. I think of the startling cleanliness of their houses and the bright chintz curtains on their windows where once were shadows of despair. I weep at their smiles of joy, their embraces, their care for others, the miracle of their deliverance in the midst of violence, stench and unbelievable squalor. I weep because I know the heart of Jesus still reaches out to the downtrodden and the despised. He was himself despised and rejected of men, a man of sorrows and acquainted with grief.

And we, who are not only in the world but of it, hide our faces from him. He is despised, and we esteem him not. And when I say "we" I include myself.

Questions for Study and Discussion

1. What distinction does the author make between patriotism and true loyalty? Discuss how patriotism is essentially a worldly attitude.

2. "Loyalty refuses either to abandon its country in its difficulties or to tolerate its sins and weaknesses." If this statement is true, what logical steps must we take in response?

3. How does Peter's reminder in 1 Peter 3:3-4 effectively combat the tendency to worldly emphases in Christians' clothing? What makes a woman truly attractive? Why?

4. How is the focus of our lives reflected in our plans for retirement? Does a Christian ever earn "the right" to take it easy?

5. How has the entertainment or propaganda model of evangelism affected the image and substance of our Christianity? Give specific examples from your own experience.

6. Prescribe a more wholesome, real, and effective emphasis for the proclamation of the gospel, based on Jesus' ministry.

7. How do evangelicals' attitudes to celebrity, success, power, size, and money reflect the world?

9

PSYCHOLOGY AS RELIGION

Worldliness attacks the church not only in the area of her carnal desires but in the realm of false philosophies. Church historians sometimes try to show the relationship between philosophy and theology. St. Thomas Aquinas, considered by many Roman Catholics to be the church's greatest theologian, was deeply influenced by Aristotle. Karl Barth, while rebelling against the old liberalism, is thought to have been influenced too much by existentialist thought. Jonathan Edwards, who was mightily used by God in the early New England revivals, has been accused by some writers of owing much of his thinking to Locke's empiricism though he was, to my mind, cleared of such charges by Harold P. Simonson in his book, *Jonathan Edwards: Theologian of the Heart* (Eerdmans, 1975). But because I am neither a theologian nor a philosopher, I do not feel qualified to speak authoritatively on such matters.

The ideas that represent the greatest threats to the church today come less from philosophy than from psychology, an area of recent study I have some understanding of, which often assumes the attributes of philosophy, though it really represents a loose kind of humanism without the rigorous and disciplined thinking of real philosophy. Indeed, I believe it is the shoddiest and cheapest forms of psychology which influence the church the most.

The swing to psychology

It is surprising that it should be so. Until about fifteen years ago psychology was seen by most Christians as hostile to the gospel. Norman Vincent Peale was perhaps the earliest professing Christian in North America to popularize psychology in the church with *The Power of Positive Thinking,* a book which awoke a certain amount of misgiving on the part of more conservative Christians. In Britain, Leslie Weatherhead exerted an influence similar to Peale's.

It is still true that many evangelical Christians are suspicious of ungodly psychologists and psychiatrists. But let someone who professes the name of Jesus baptize secular psychology and present it as something compatible with Scripture truth, and most Christians are happy to swallow theological hemlock in the form of "psychological insights."

A form of religion

The psychologies are two things. They are a science (of a sort) and they are a form of religion. I say "a form of religion" because too many people want to find in them what they once found in religious faith—a way of dealing with their failure. After all, what more could you ask for than a "religion" that is backed by science?

The parallels between the psychologies and religion grow more fascinating the more closely we look at them. Take psychoanalysis, for example. It is primarily a Jewish movement, and it incorporates many of the features of Judaism. The psychoanalyst is the rabbi. The whole training of analysts is a strange blend of the rabbinical system and cabalistic traditions. There are the usual sectarian rivalries among different schools of analysis; some are orthodox and cling to Freud; others are modernists and go after the ego psychologists. There is also the adulation, the profound respect amounting almost to worship, the serious and careful analysis of everything the latest chief rabbi (the outstandingly popular psychoanalyst) says. It may be pure gibberish. But never was gibberish discussed with such earnest solemnity and credulity.

I am exaggerating, of course. It would be foolish to pretend that the movement is entirely nonsensical, or entirely Jewish. But what is true of psychoanalysis is true of all the psychologies. Skinner, with his *Walden Two*, has proclaimed behavioral psychology to be the savior of the world and the basis of a new utopia. So whether we are dealing with Gestalt psychology, behaviorism, or psychoanalysis, it is all one in promising more than it can deliver. If this were not so, why is there always a need for new schools, offering "ultimate" solutions?

Psychology or Scripture?

Who gets the good jobs in the big city churches? The man with a D.Min. in counselling. Over the past fifteen years there has been a tendency for churches to place increasing reliance on trained pastoral counselors. I cannot help but wonder whether the shift in emphasis is not a dangerous one. To me it seems to suggest weaknesses in or indifference to expository preaching within evangelical churches. What has real godly counselling to do with pop psychology? Why are the Scriptures ignored in the counselor's office? Why do we have to turn to the human sciences at all? Why? Because for years we have failed to expound the whole of Scripture. Because from our weakened exposition and our superficial topical talks we have produced a generation of Christian sheep having no shepherd. And now we are damning ourselves more deeply than ever by our recourse to the wisdom of the world.

How can I remain a psychiatrist and spout such "heresy"? Well, a psychiatrist is simply a doctor—a doctor who treats mental diseases, many of which are associated with disordered brain chemistry. In saying this I do not despise the serious and valuable work of my psychologist colleagues. My point is that what I do as a psychiatrist and what my psychologist colleagues do in their researches or their counselling is of infinitely less value to distressed Christians than what God says in his Word. But pastoral shepherds, like the sheep they guide, are following (if I may change my metaphor for a moment) a new Pied Piper of Hamlin who is leading them into the dark caves of humanistic hedonism.

It troubles me that Christian counselors trained to the doctoral level should have their clinical training under the supervision of secular psychologists in secular universities, many of whom are soaked in pop psychology. My own contact with such counselors, while not extensive, is sufficient to convince me that Christian counselors are influenced more than they realize by such psychology which, besides being shoddy, is at its roots profoundly anti-Christian in a deeper sense than either psychoanalysis or behaviorism. I believe it is essential that psychologies of any brand be subjected to the most rigorous examination in the light of Scripture, especially those psychologies which would be termed pop psychology.

I am also appalled at the way Christian authors adopt such humanistic and hedonistic principles, glorify them with a few out of context verses of Scripture, and dish them up to the Christian public. A few of us who are deeply involved in the human sciences feel like voices crying in a godless wilderness of humanism, while the churches turn to humanistic psychology as a substitute for the gospel of God's grace. My rage and despair are often inexpressible. *In* the world? In the area of human sciences the church is rapidly becoming *of* it and of its most damnable and destructive doctrines.

The cult of self-worship

I am grateful to Professor Paul Vitz for alerting me to the specific dangers of this particular fashion in psychotherapy in his book *Psychology as Religion* (Eerdmans, 1977). Vitz, a New York psychologist, coins the term *selfism*, by which he means preoccupation with one's own ego, one's personal fulfillment and the pampering that one demands in the name of self-worth. Associated with this preoccupation is the idea that one should learn to be nonjudgmental towards oneself, "warts and all."

Embracing Bertrand Russell's atheistic stance as a student, Vitz slowly came to a realization of the truth of Christianity in 1972. In his book he vigorously attacks humanistic "self-psychology" and, though he does not embark on a critique of psychoanalytic theory or behaviorism, he does point out that "many American psychoanalysts have accepted so much of self-psychology that it is difficult to identify them as Freudian at all. Likewise, behavior modification therapists frequently expose various self-actualizing philosophies in their own lives and as part of their professional ethic."

I agree with Vitz that one of the great enemies today, both of Christian doctrine and of vital Christian living, is a humanistic self-psychology. Its stance is man-centered, anti-Christian and socially dangerous. Vitz quotes Donald Campbell who, as president of the American Psychological Association, stated, "There is in psychology today a general background assumption that the human impulses provided by biological evolution are right and optimal, both individually and socially, and that repressive or inhibitory moral traditions are wrong. This assumption may now be regarded as scientifically wrong. Psychology, in propagating this background perspective in its teaching of perhaps 80 to 90 percent of college undergraduates, and increasing proportions of high school and elementary school pupils, helps to undermine the retention of what may be extremely valuable social-evolutionary inhibiting systems which we do not yet fully understand."

While he does not go along with greater self-control for religious reasons, Campbell is saying that the concepts of sin and the fall of man are *socially necessary*. They help us to understand our destructive behavior for what it is and to put a check on unbridled hedonism. His ideas are remarkable in the light of his personal world-view. Campbell views human society through evolutionary spectacles. Yet he believes that there is "social functionality and psychological validity to the concepts of sin and temptation and of original sin due to human carnal, animal nature." Many Christian psychologists who would indignantly deny the evolutionary perspective from which Campbell speaks nevertheless embrace the principles of the pop psychology, that he has rejected on the basis of logic.

The attraction of a "selfist" philosophy for Christian counselors lies in its apparent offer to free legalistic Christians from the hang-ups and inhibitions that arise from mistaken ideas of what God requires of us. But the leap from legalism over to selfism can be a leap into ever-increasing and uncontrolled license.

In *Psychology as Religion*, Vitz sees the fathers of selfist psychology as Eric Fromm, Carl Rogers, Abraham Maslow, and Rollo May. He points out that their ideas were far from new, and notes the curious coincidence that three of the four graduated from Columbia Teachers' College (where all of them studied under a prominent disciple of Thomas Dewey) and two of them are graduates of Union Theological Seminary. In turn, they were followed by a group of lesser gurus—Eric Berne,

Thomas Harris, Nathaniel Branden, Alex Comfort and others, the popularizers of pop psychology and a generation which journalists of the 70s called the *me generation*. Vitz discusses the theological shallowness that failed to perceive the incongruity of transactional analysis and selfism with Christianity.

The religion of selfism

The title of one of Branden's books will be a good starting point for a discussion on selfism: *The Psychology of Self Esteem*. Self-esteem means (roughly) feeling good about yourself. It corresponds to the "I'm O.K." of Harris's *I'm O.K.—You're O.K.* A closely related idea is self-love. I am not surprised at the confusion that has arisen among Christians about self-love and self-esteem. At first glance they seem to exemplify Christian principles. How can we love our neighbors *as ourselves* unless we love ourselves? How can we suffer from poor esteem if we are children of the King of kings? Let us examine both ideas more carefully. Though they appear innocuous, if not actually Christian, they represent the entranceway into a view of man that is anti-God and anti-Christ.

To despise oneself and to hate oneself are painful experiences. It is very understandable, when we despise ourselves, to long for escape through the gateway of self-esteem; or when we hate ourselves, to yearn to discover something likeable, even lovable about ourselves. Both self-esteem and self-hatred can be a part of profound depression, and whatever view one may take of depression, all of us recognize that it is undesirable.

But is high self-esteem the opposite of low self-esteem?

If the words mean what they seem to mean one would think so. Yet what are we taught in the New Testament about self esteem? "For by grace given me I say," Paul writes, "Do not think of yourself more highly than you ought, but rather think of yourself with sober judgment, in accordance with the measure of faith God has given you" (Rom. 12:3 NIV). The Christian ideal is not that we replace poor self-esteem with high self-esteem, but with realistic self-appraisal. And what is realistic self-appraisal?

I suppose realistic self-appraisal is based first on a correct perception of our relationship with God and, second, on a correct perception of our relation with fellow humans, particularly fellow Christians. Though sin has marred me terribly, yet I am at worst the wreck of something that God created in his very image. If I am a wreck, then I am the wreck of something noble and beautiful. I am also his redeemed and adopted child. So while I may be unworthy of the honor he does me, nevertheless (and I will grasp this concept "in accordance with the measure of faith God has given" me) I am set apart for his sole use, an object of a rescue attempt that meant the incarnation, death, and resurrection of Christ, and the ongoing indwelling presence of the Holy Spirit. I am being changed into Christ's image "from glory to glory," that is, from one degree of glory to another. *To grasp such truths is to be filled with awe and wonder* at God's astonishing kindness, an experience far, far removed from the psychological concept of self-esteem.

While no one seems to make it explicit, self-esteem is really based on a comparison of ourselves with others, a comparison Paul avoided. "We do not dare," he writes, "to classify or compare ourselves with some who commend themselves. When they compare themselves with themselves"—a form of elitism—"they are not wise" (2 Cor. 10:12 NIV).

The Christian view of self

How, then, should we Christians view ourselves? Clearly (and this is the context in which Paul writes in Romans 12) we are all essential parts of one body. We are needed, not because we are more important than others, but because we are just as important to them as they are to us. While this may not be apparent, since other people's gifts often seem more spectacular than our own, nevertheless the Holy Spirit has a different scale of values than we have and urges us to fully use those gifts God has given us to build up the body of Christ (Rom. 12:4-8).

I must confess that I find that Paul's instructions go against my natural grain and that I seem to oscillate between fantasies of the applause and admiration I would like to receive from my friends, and self-disgust when I realize how poor my gifts seem when compared with others'. To be truthful, I know that my carnal self shares with Satan the ambition to supercede everybody and everything in the universe. I rarely permit myself to see this, but I know it to be true. But I also know that along that route lies no peace. My peace and my joy come from realizing how wonderful, how unspeakably marvelous, is God's grace to me, and how the Holy Spirit brings me constantly into contact with people with a wide variety of gifts—*every one of them necessary to my own happiness.* But I need the Holy Spirit to open my eyes to my fellow believers and to see them from God's perspective. Only when this is true does this precious concept begin to warm my heart with Christian love and praise.

I have failed, so far, to explain how loving one's neighbor as oneself (Mark 12:23) can be incompatible with self-love. Everything depends on how we define self-love. The phrase means different things in different contexts. When Christ used the expression, he was talking about behavior rather than emotion. He was encouraging us to treat our neighbors with the same degree of consideration that we give to ourselves, to be as concerned with their problems as with our own and express that concern in action. Behavior of that kind does not spring from self-love as it is conceived of today, but from a grateful awareness of how much God loves me, and from a response of love to God on my part. Such love enables me to see my neighbors through God's eyes, to treat them as God would treat them, and in the same way as God treats me. It is an outflowing of the love of God.

Self-love, as conceived by selfist psychology, leads to self-gratification, to an ever-increasing preoccupation with self-fulfillment in areas such as sensuality, acquisitiveness, competition, and the exercise of power. This trend has become explicit only during the past decade. Nevertheless, the trend is the logical conclusion of the false premise. Far from being an aid to loving my neighbor, self-love is that which leads in the end to riding roughshod over him, trampling him to death if need be. Even if my sensual delights call for sado-masochism or any other form of sensual perversion, then I should not deny myself such delights. Gradually the cycle becomes complete. Self-love in this sense is self-lust—the lust of the flesh, the lust of the eyes and the pride of life, none of which are of the Father but of this world and are symptomatic of the hedonistic age in which we live. It is worldly, thoroughly worldly, in the most biblical sense of the term. But Christian counselors would never admit (or would they?) that, logically, hedonism must follow "self-love" as defined by selfist psychologists.

I would be the last person to dismiss the findings of psychologists, sociologists, anthropologists, or of my colleagues in psychiatry. All of us are interested in the human being. Insofar as we are truly scientific we shall not go far wrong (even though we will always fall short of true understanding), for we will discover some of the marvels of God's creativity in the production of his masterpiece—a being created in time and space, made in his very image. Thus it is not against the scientific exploration I protest; scientific experimentation and analysis may sharpen our insights and challenge some notions which we have falsely assumed to be biblical. But I object to the cheap and shoddy pseudophilosophies arising from inaccurate observations, pseudophilosophies that pander to the worship of man and gratification of our selfish desires. Selfist psychology is a wolf in sheep's clothing. It should be rooted out of our lives, its books tossed into our garbage pails, and its use in Christian counseling replaced by counsel that is truly biblical and God-honoring.

Questions for Study and Discussion
1. What kinds of psychology seem to affect the church the most? Why do you think this is true?

2. Describe some of the parallels between religion and psychology. Where do both fail?

3. Why does the author believe that Christians have forsaken God's wisdom and looked to the wisdom of the world (the psychologies) for life's answers?

4. Why are the concepts of man's sin and failure socially necessary, from a psychological stand-point? From a Christian standpoint?

5. What is the logical result of the leap from legalism to selfism? Where is a truer liberation to be found?

6. Describe how selfism is both anti-God and anti-Christ.

7. On what is realistic self-appraisal based? Where does our true importance lie?

10

THE TRUMPET WITH THE UNCERTAIN SOUND

GOD'S PEOPLE HAVE BEEN CHEATED AND ROBBED—cheated and robbed of the truth of Scripture. I may exaggerate a little, but there is rock-bottom truth in what I say. In the twentieth century, throughout the English-speaking world, the Bible truth has been taught inadequately. It has been partially and unevenly taught. Certain aspects have been emphasized at the expense of others. Some things which are pure lies are taught as exciting truths.

An example is in the area of fund-raising. God *does* reward our giving, sometimes in this life and sometimes in the next. But from Christian telethons comes the message "Give to us, and God will make you rich!" Such distortions of biblical truth would never dominate the Christian scene to the extent that they do if Scripture had been thoroughly and systematically taught.

Oh, doctrine has been taught, but selectively, the main emphasis being on the Pauline epistles. Justification has been curiously divorced from sanctification. Holiness has been presented as a special doctrine for selected Christians instead of God's stringent demand (is he not a holy God?) for all his people; he who justifies also sanctifies. Preachers have preached what people have wanted to hear—that in effect they can justify themselves before God by "victorious Christian living." I know that the matter has not been expressed so blatantly, nevertheless that is how the message has been picked up and applied by those who listened. I have already complained about topical preachers and preaching. It has led to an anemic, feeble church with no idea what worldliness is all about, so that worldliness is seen as anything that is, at the moment, unfashionable with Christians.

Jesus wept? Jesus weeps.

He weeps over sheep fed on lollipops, while the Word of God, the whole Word of God, is edited and reduced to a few favorite passages—Psalm 23, John 3, 1 Corinthians 13 (sentimentally presented and seldom properly examined or expounded), the Galatian epistle, and the book of Revelation (with explanatory charts). Of course, the Sermon on the Mount has been deleted (we are good dispensationalists and have no room for "kingdom legalism").

So Jesus weeps. His very words are being ignored.

He weeps over poor, deceived young people who are falsely taught by enthusiastic preachers that an instant, subjective experience at a special conference will solve all their problems and give them a zippy, automatic, Christian joy for the rest of their lives. Garbage! Lying and devilish garbage—that leads young Christians to despair, to frustration, and to the terrible sense that if things go wrong, God has abandoned them or they have failed. You meant no harm, preacher, but why did you go on preaching about victory when your own life lacked it? It is a serious thing to mislead young and old alike with a distorted gospel. You may one day be called to account for all those lies you so sincerely outlined at Bible conferences, and all those easy promises about abundant life.

Real Christian growth is slow and painful. It is not an "experience," though it may continue through many experiences. It may begin with repentance and commitment, but that commitment must be learned and adhered to as a daily, life-long discipline. It will need all the support and patient counsel that godly counselors can give.

What does the trumpet signal?

One reason behind the new worldliness is that the trumpet has sounded not only an uncertain but an arrantly false note.

I sit writing in the middle of a gambling casino. (Why? I can't find anywhere else to sit just now and the air conditioning is on.) It is a crazy place where people seek amusement in what can never give them joy. I am under no illusion. I know where I am. I *expect* the devil to deceive people here. But when God's people—that is, Christian preachers—organize holiday camps where they profess to teach truth and actually teach what is just as false as the lure of the gambling casino, I am enraged! Some such camps (certainly not all) offer the comfort of tobacco-free golf. Others segregate us from the offense of profanity. They teach a religion of experiences and thrills, of a sanctification divorced from justification. Perhaps the Christian nightclub movement is over now. While it lasted it offered Christian artists and nonalcoholic beverages. And my dear Lord Jesus weeps!

Yet perhaps the camps were necessary. At least they sought to teach Scripture when the churches were failing to do so. God has used them. The churches were not giving people hope; but ultimately, the short-term camps and conferences represented only a band aid approach to Christian teaching. In the postwar years, Christianity has become increasingly a holiday religion, proclaimed wherever sun and sermons can lure sanctification-seekers in the belief that a Christian holiday combines fun and godliness. But in the eyes of the world there is no difference between a Christian holiday camp and any other kind. Once again, we are being *of* the world as well as in it.

Where do we go to learn godliness?
I have no doubt that God has used conference organizers and speakers. They have met a need when spiritual life was at a low ebb. But the local church is the place where godliness must be learned, not the holiday camp. And if the local congregation is not doing what it should, then the Christian holiday camp never will! All it can provide is a temporary Christian "high," a mild form of "spiritual" entertainment that will tickle the appetites of bored Christians from dead churches and lure them into the

false hope of a new relationship with God. In the mercy of God, such temporary ministry has done more good than harm. But why do the same people need to go back year after year? Are they really growing in grace? Or do they return to recapture a "truth" that repeatedly eludes them in real life?

What note should the trumpet sound?

There are no shortcuts to holiness. There is no easy way to conquer the flesh. Christian character is a matter of growth, not of secrets or formulas. Growth takes time. It also takes the discipline of prayer, of study, of heart searching, of sensitivity to the Holy Ghost's pleading, and of consistent obedience. We live in an age of instant coffee and fast food joints. But there is no instant solution to carnality. It must always begin with a renewed awareness of our sin, a daily renewed thankfulness for the never-ending grace of God, and a sense of being set free repeatedly to a life of holiness.

I suppose there is much to be said for a personal systematic study of the whole body of Scripture. But that takes time—a long time. I've tried it and I know. It took me ten years to get through Philippians, Galatians, Romans 1-8, the first part of Acts, Nehemiah, Hosea, sections of Isaiah, Revelation, Philemon and the Sermon on the Mount. (Oh, and my favorite selection of other chapters from the Bible.) I dread to think how long it would take me to get through the whole Bible. It took Martyn Lloyd-Jones two years to study Matthew 5, 6, and 7!

No. I suppose what are needed are men and women of God, in touch with both the contemporary culture and the Spirit of God, who will explain and teach those undealt-with sections of the Scripture so specially needed by the people of God. Such an individual was the late Fred Mitchell, the home director of what was then the China Inland Mission. I was still a medical student when he died in a plane crash, but always he had seemed to me to be God's man, saying God's Word to God's people at God's time.

I wept when he died. Why did God take him when he was so desperately needed? I knelt by my bedside crying inconsolably as I prayed that God would raise up seven men to take Fred Mitchell's place. And then, deeply concerned that God answer my prayer, I was bold enough to ask God to consider making me one of the seven. I knew I could never be half the man Fred Mitchell was, but I was willing to struggle along in his steps.

What then must we do? We must stop assuming that all Christian believers are such simpletons that they will be bored by expository and doctrinal preaching. While it is true that not all preachers are able to make expository preaching vital and relevant, and that others deliver doctrinal addresses as though they were lecturing in a classroom, exposition rightly delivered, and doctrine rightly explained, will satisfy the deepest cravings of Christian spirits for truth.

True exposition, rightly understood, reduces itself to three simple steps. First, the text must be *examined* closely with the preacher pointing out what the passage says as well as what it doesn't say. Second, its meaning must be *explained* logically and lucidly. Congregations are not made up of morons, nor do they come to be entertained. They need systematic instruction. Finally, what is explained must be *applied*. The preacher must follow these three basic steps, discussing what the passage says, what it means, and how it is relevant in today's situation.

Why is this simple approach largely ignored? I suspect it is because preachers either underestimate the intelligence and spiritual hunger of their congregations, or else because the preachers themselves have never discovered the wonder, depth, and joy of Scriptural truth.

Admittedly, doctrine is more difficult. But once again we insult and deprive Christian people by treating them as children. Doctrine must be taught systematically and thoroughly from the pulpit. It is a tragic mistake to suppose that theology must be taught only to seminary students. To whom did Paul write his doctrinal letters? To seminaries or to local churches?

Here, then, is my first practical suggestion to stem the tide of worldliness in the church. *Let preachers expound Scripture again!* Let them expend the time and effort to *teach biblical doctrine!* Let them forget their anecdotal, topical, shallow sermonettes. Let them preach the Word of God! Any preacher who systematically teaches the truth of the Scriptures will find people coming to hear him. God's people are spiritually starved and will be drawn to the meat of the Word as bees to honey. When expounded prayerfully, systematically, and in the Spirit's power, God's Word will call God's people back to repentance, prayer, and renewed faith in himself. But it demands faith to believe that you don't have to run the church like a circus in order to attract people, nor import big name speakers at fancy prices. The Word of God is powerful enough in itself, and the Word alone attracts. Don't ever try to defend it. Expound it!

But, and here I address preachers, don't ever preach a

Scripture truth that is foreign to your own experience. Don't preach theoretical truth to a hungry congregation. As you study, pray that God will make the passage living and real in your own experience. Obey what God is saying *to you* and your sermons will have the authenticity of practice rather than the tentativeness of theory.

Preach from the prophets! Preach from the book of Job! Preach from those parts of Scripture you have never heard anyone else preach from! Preach from the Gospels. Preach from the books of Leviticus and Deuteronomy. Let no area of Scripture be excluded!

Preach simply. Make the truth clear enough for a twelve-year-old to grasp. Preach plainly. Preach with conviction. Preach lovingly. And let one of your prayers be that God will raise up from the midst of your congregation those who will be even better preachers than you yourself are.

But how can that happen?

Questions for Study and Discussion

1. To what basic lack does the author attribute the uncertainty and superficiality of twentieth century Christianity?

2. What do today's preachers emphasize? Why? What do they neglect? Why?

3. Why is the definition "worldliness is . . . anything that is, at the moment, unfashionable with Christians" a misleading one?

4. If "there is no instant solution to carnality," what does it take for a Christian to change and mature spiritually?

5. What are the three levels of Scripture exposition? Why is each level important?

11
HOW CHRISTIANS
CAN CHANGE
& GROW

WE HAVE SEEN HOW EASILY WORLDLINESS arises from unfamiliarity with (and thus disobedience to) the Word of God. But worldliness among Christians also results from the irrelevance of church structures.

How is the average church organized?

Briefly it is a matter of who does the organizing and who are the organized. We pay pastors to preside over our religious instruction and observance. This divides the church into professionals and amateurs, or powerful church boards and passive pew warmers. And the only answer that seems to occur to us as we perceive the trouble and distress of the sheep is to hire *another* professional—a well-qualified pastoral counselor.

Where, in the average church, is there an opportunity for troubled church members to discuss their real problems and concerns? In what forum may they discuss their marital conflicts, their problem children, the ethical problems that arise in their jobs? (Oh, I know they are "organized." Organized into Sunday school teachers, presidents of youth groups, secretaries of young marrieds, or singles groups. Most churches are superbly organized clubs, and in this, too, they are of the world.)

But where may members meet to "let their hair down," to pray for one another, to personally study Scripture? Many churches are beginning to recognize the need for their members to pray together, to study together and to provide understanding and mutual support—burden-bearing—for one another. Here and there in this continent cell groups, also known as growth groups or fellowship groups, are developing, with or without the consent of the ecclesiastical hierarchy.

Often a problem arises where cell groups begin to form in a church community. Church members have limited free time. You cannot attend a weekly prayer-fellowship/Bible study group and continue to support the ladies' fellowship, (or the men's Bible study program), the college and career group, choir practice, Sunday school teachers' meeting, and a full schedule of Sunday services. Something has to give. Unhappily, the professionals (I mean those in the full-time pastorate), because they fear things may go out of control, usually have a bias towards the more conventional groupings in the traditional church organizations, so that what the Holy Spirit is striving to teach them may be ignored.

Why can we not learn common sense? How can we be

so blind to our deep needs and to God's answers to those needs? We must face facts squarely and decide, both on the congregational and leadership levels, what are our most important priorities.

What should a small fellowship group do? What functions ought it to fulfill? Let me list what I see as its most important areas of benefit:

1. It is an arena, regularly available, for sharing both problems and praise, and for mutual prayer support.

2. It encourages personal holiness, discipline, and growth.

3. It provides a context for systematic, small group inductive Bible study.

4. It promotes the learning and practice of true worship, in song and/or prayer.

5. It allows for unself-conscious, practical (financial) caring for personal needs.

6. It breaks down barriers that often divide churches into cliques.

7. It encourages the development of new leadership and the exercise of spiritual gifts.

You can readily see that it is logistically impossible to meet the needs suggested by this list in a church numbering over fifty persons without the intimacy of small groups. The larger the group, the harder it is for everyone to hear, and the more scary it becomes for timid people to take part. Thus, the larger the church, the more impossible it is to share on a real, personal and edifying level. And as support groups form it is clearly desirable for each to maintain vital contact with church leaders who, if they are any good at their job, will visit such groups regularly if not be a part of one.

Permit me to enlarge on some of the advantages of intimate fellowship.

First, group members will discover that they are each a part of a caring, praying "family." They will frequently telephone one another during the week to share urgent or special prayer needs, or answers. This new sense of family will develop among the group members and draw them into real "body life." People discover that their problems are not unique. Others are facing similar difficulties, or have lived through them and learned spiritual principles in the process.

Second, a covenant or agreement may develop among the members to encourage one another's personal holiness. Too often, when we use the term "discipline" it has negative connotations that suggest dealing firmly, even harshly, with the wrong-doing of a group member. But by church discipline I mean mutual edification, "building up" and training in positive Christian living.

A small group provides a number of advantages for such discipline. First it demonstrates this positive aspect of discipline—mutual nurturing and positive help in an atmosphere of trust and confidentiality among all the group members. This will take time, but loving admonition, mutual prayer, and caring, loving inquiry into one another's spiritual problems, a new openness—all these will create the environment in which what one might call "negative" discipline, (the correction of wrong-doing) can take place. Unless both positive and negative aspects are present, discipline will be unhelpful and disruptive. But the atmosphere must not be forced. People must have the freedom either to remain silent or to speak.

The larger church body cannot provide this context.

In the first place, the logistics of such caring and sharing, to say nothing of the embarrassment church members feel about baring their souls in a large group, all inhibit mutual caring and prayer. One reason that church discipline has been so signal a failure is that it has been separated from a greater whole—the tender, mutual, loving commitment to holy living in a small group.

Third, inductive Bible study is best practiced in small groups. Clearly a good leader is needed—one who will not preach, nor arrive with an armload of commentaries and Bible dictionaries, but will have the quiet skill of spotting the key points in a passage, and of asking the right kind of questions (Who? What? Why? etc.) that will lead the whole group to discuss essential details. With such a leader, it is surprising how quickly members will begin to grasp that they, too, can get something out of Bible study, can even learn to study and understand the Bible for themselves!

A number of excellent inductive Bible study programs for church, home, or student use are now available. I recommend Fisherman Bible Studyguides, a series of Bible book and topical studies published by Harold Shaw Publishers for small groups. InterVarsity Press also produces inductive studyguides. Both series are being widely used among thoughtful Christians in churches and homes under the leadership of the Holy Spirit. Also, Carpenter Studyguides (Harold Shaw) offer inductive Bible study along with other elements geared to small groups within a church.

Fourth, in small groups, people can learn true worship. Worship? But, you may say, in our big church there *is* real worship; you should hear our choir! Is that real worship? Or is "worship" confined to singing certain hymns, listening to the pastor pray, and offering the worship of our tithes and offerings in the plates that are passed round? To learn worship (God's worth-ship) we must join others in ascribing worth to God in small groups. True healing discipline and true worship both begin there. A time may be set aside for quiet thankfulness and adoration. Men and women who would never dare to pray extemporaneously in a large congregation can begin to stumble through their first expressions of praise and love to Christ. Indeed, such should be one of the group's aims. Simple Scripture songs which express thanks or praise to God will help unite the group in corporate worship and may either set the tone for individual sentence prayers of praise, or conclude such a session.

Fifth, members will begin to discover one another's needs. A man has lost a job. A mother needs a babysitter so that she can earn much-needed income. Sickness in a member's home can provide an opportunity for others to bring in hot meals for the family. Such mutual aid is far more natural in a small group than in a large church. Even financial sharing will begin to take place—not on a commune principle, but as a glad and private giving and receiving of personal resources.

Sixth, groups should be heterogeneous, including young and old, men and women, couples and singles, sophisticated and simple, educated and uneducated. This may at first seem to impede the progress of the group. Yet it is the only way that all can become one in Christ and begin to learn from one another. The great resources of the church lie dormant at present because of the walls of distrust and lack of understanding in the body of Christ.

Seventh, new spiritual leaders will arise. Gifts which could never have had opportunity for exercise in the large congregation will quickly begin to be demonstrated in the smaller group. A new spiritual, pastoral ministry will begin to manifest itself as new elders will grow and be recognized.

Now, I realize that some of these developments may constitute a threat to the "professional" leadership. I also realize that groups can get off on some tangent or even into doctrinal heresy. But anything that is good has its disadvantages and dangers, and unless we take risks we will never make progress. If ever there is to be something that the world will recognize as not *of* itself, it will be the phenomenon of Christians meeting to pray and to love one another in a practical way. It is not the big, well-dressed Sunday morning congregational service that attracts sinners but the warm fellowship of the house group. I have seen neighbors drop by and become soundly converted when they see Christian life and love in action.

Two of the biggest mistakes in church strategy are those that seem to produce the biggest churches. The first is the aggressive bussing of children to Sunday School, and the second is the segregation of social classes and cultural traditions. Both methods work, and work exceedingly well—if by success we mean bigness and prosperity.

But do size and success matter to Christ? Not according to the letter to Laodicea, where Christ condemns those who say "I am rich, I have prospered, and

I need nothing" (Rev. 3:17). What matters to Christ is the growth of members of his body in holiness, love, and grace. As in our TV success story, so in the increase in church budget and church membership, size impresses non-Christians in the wrong way. The response of the worldly individual is likely to be, "Well, it's not my personal thing—but these folk surely know how to organize." The glory does not go to God but to the organizational efficiency of the church leaders.

Don't misunderstand me. Don't interpret my remarks to represent an attack on bigness in itself, or that God in his grace is not at work in large churches. People are being converted in them. A work of God is often going on in them. But because God is not perceived by non-Christians as the power behind the success, the success may be only partial and may be thought of as being no different from that of other clubs and associations. The good is once again the enemy of the best in two of the most critical needs of the church today—the need for discipline (in the broad sense mentioned earlier) and the need for true spiritual worship.

But, how . . . ?

What can be done to change the structure of churches, to promote more group Bible study, small group prayer, the development of spiritual gifts? How may we foster godly, caring discipline and the feeling of family in the anonymity of the larger church?

First, we must individually and corporately seek God's face. It may be that there are deeper, more radical needs than organizing churches into small home groups. We must beware of hailing them simply as the latest fad in church renewal. There may be bitterness and hatred among members, in the church. Perhaps there are rivalries and jealousies of long standing. Or there may be sins among the leadership, sins of pride or doubt or immorality that need to be repented of and put right. Where God has convicted me of hatred I must not go to the person involved and blurt out, "I have always hated you!" It will take the love of God in me to say, simply, "I have had a wrong attitude toward you, and God has shown me my sin. I know I have his forgiveness now, but I would like yours as well. Will you forgive me?"

Let those within the church who are deeply concerned meet for regular prayer and waiting upon God. Let our prayers not merely cover the usual range of our prayer requests, but be a seeking of God's face, an earnest cry to him to show us our needs, our sins, and our weaknesses. We may be surprised that God is more ready to hear us than we are to pray! In fact, whenever we pray like this it is he who has drawn us to himself, drawn us because he wanted to commune with us. Let us wait on him, not confusing the stillness of his presence with the deadly monotony of routine.

And as God begins to teach us, we need to ask him whether ideas like house groups are part of his plan for our church. Let us study Scripture together, and read books like *The Problem of Wineskins*, *The Community of the King* and *The Radical Wesley* by Howard Snyder. Let us study works such as *The Dynamics of Spiritual Renewal* by Richard Lovelace and *Body Life* by Ray Stedman.

After such prayer and study, God may lead us to take action. We will need to ask questions like these: Along what lines should we form groups? What about the inevitable competition for time and interest between house groups and more traditional weekly activities? How should groups be related to the church and to its formal leaders? What degree of autonomy should each group have? Ought we to make groups a voluntary activity for those interested, or should all church members be expected and encouraged to participate? Who will act as Bible study leaders? (Here I must be dogmatic: the leaders should be *only* those whom God has given the gift of leading well.) How should the Bible study in groups relate to the Sunday morning worship? (It is amazing how much more alive the Scripture becomes when, after having studied a passage, one hears that same passage expounded from the pulpit the following Sunday!)

I do not know God's blueprint for renewal in your congregation. I do know that it must begin with prayer. And that prayer may need to continue for weeks and months. The questions I have asked are not academic but vital, but God must answer them for you, not I. Just as there are no two identical snowflakes, so also there are no two identical blueprints for rescuing your church from worldliness.

God knows what you need. Come before him in prayer and he will tell you where to begin.

Questions for Study and Discussion

1. Why is the division of churches into professionals and amateurs (clergy and laity) a self-defeating maneuver?

2. List the benefits of Bible study and fellowship groups within the church. What needs do such groups fill? Which of these needs is apparent in your church?

3. Why may such small groups threaten the "professionals" in a church?

4. In the author's view, what elements are included in "discipline"? Discuss how each of these elements fulfills the basic meaning of the root word.

5. Why is real discipline difficult in the context of a large congregation?

6. What are the advantages of membership in a large church? In a small fellowship? Which of these factors are important to Jesus Christ? To needy individuals?

12

TO WHOM DO WE GIVE OUR LOYALTY?

T WO QUESTIONS HAVE BEEN UPPERMOST in my mind as I have been writing this book. The first concerns how we can live *in the world* without being *part of it.* The second expresses the same thought in another way. How can we and ought we to differ from the world?

I have looked at two major reasons for our worldliness, the absence of biblical preaching, and the inappropriateness of size as a criterion of success in church organizations. I have also considered the cataract of trashy "Christian" literature, Christian films and TV programs, and their open acceptance of humanistic and hedonistic ideas.

I have pointed out that we are of the world and like the

world when we share the world's values—making physical pleasure too important, collecting beautiful clothes, homes, cars and whatever, and above all by our desire to surpass others and make them admire us. We are worldly when we lust carnally, when we crave and live for possessions and raise our proud heads above others. Please understand that I am not against pleasure or possessions or excellence. *I am against clinging to them.* The distinction is an important one and we need godly honesty with ourselves in searching our hearts.

I have shown how we are like the world when we compete with either the world or our Christian neighbors in the race for nicer homes and more fashionable clothes. We are of the world when, as Christian organizations, we adopt the world's organizational philosophies and promotional techniques. We are of the world whenever we strain at gnats and swallow camels.

I have suggested some practical remedies, but in concluding, I would like to deal with the issue of personal worldliness and how we may prevent or avoid it in the first place. What if preaching stays superficial and the same inappropriate church organizations continue to exist. What then can you and I do on the individual level?

First we must repent. Before God, we must ask his Spirit to search our hearts. "Search me, O God, and know my heart; test me and know my anxious thoughts. See if there is any offensive way in me, and lead me in the way everlasting" (Psalm 139:23-24 NIV). Heartsearching and repentance must precede any action.

God will not fail you if you come before him individually, just as I urged a congregation to do a few pages back. Changes that are not rooted in repentance and prayer will be mere gimmickry, shallow and temporary at best. We are obsessed in the West with the easy how-to's of success. Is there a problem? Let us figure out the simple solution—and voilà—problem solved!

But in the affairs of God it does not work like that. The work is not ours, but his. And he cannot work with us in the way he wishes to unless we take the time to wait in silence upon him. First he needs to bring our hearts to the point where we begin to share his viewpoint. Then, we must *persist* in following after him.

Will you pray, along with me, "Dear Lord, show me myself. Tell me where I grieve you. I feel within me the pull of the world and I am both ashamed and weak. I *want* to obey you and yet I find myself craving the things the world offers as well.

"Lord, make Heaven *real* to me. Teach me to know at the very center of my being that my true citizenship is in heaven, not here on earth. Thank you for the material blessings you have poured on me, but tear the attraction for them from my heart so that I become truly indifferent to wealth, or poverty, and am free to abound or to be in want, indifferent to every circumstance in life except only that I may hold your hand and walk beside you. Show me that the world is a fickle and false companion, and a cruel master. Keep me loyal to you.

"Draw me back into the conflict and teach me to equip myself like a soldier. Deliver me from that kind of retirement that is meaningless and selfish. Show me now, before I retire, while I am still young, how you want me to use my home. Give me wisdom to know whether I should invite others in to pray and study your Word with them. Help me to teach my children by my attitude to possessions that this world's riches mean nothing, but that heavenly riches mean everything.

"Deliver me from the lure of TV commercials, or mail advertising. Free me from all the inducement to acquire which bombards me on every side.

"Teach me not to make a god of my bodily passions. Teach me to eat, to drink, to sleep and, if I am married, to make love thankfully and with gratitude to you. Deliver me from marital conflict, and should it arise, lead me to deeper understanding and appreciation of my mate. Grant that I may never even mention the word divorce, and reinforce me against the subtle attraction to another's spouse.

"Teach me to be poor in spirit, to mourn, to be meek and to hunger and thirst after righteousness. You told me I am light; place me where I may shine for you. You told me to be salt; preserve my saltiness and let it be felt by those I come in contact with.

"Show me the difference between gnats and camels, between what is merely the product of an ingrown Christian culture and what is truly important.

"Dear Lord, it seems to me that the time may be short. Hire me like one of those laborers hired at the eleventh hour that I too may labor in your harvest field.

"Blessed be your name, O Lord. Let your kingdom come quickly. And so awaken me by your spirit that my lamp may be burning when you, my lover, my heavenly husband, arrive to claim me as your bride.

"Even so, come, Lord Jesus."

Questions for Study and Discussion

1. What major causes does the author see for worldly Christians? Which of these has affected you, personally?

2. What turns a good or useful thing into an idol?

3. What suggestions does the author make to help us change and grow as individual believers?

4. Why are repentance and persistence never easy? Why are both essential for real Christian growth and change?

5. As you have read this book, at what points have you admitted, "Yes. He's talking about me. I needed that reminder"? Focus now on those worldly inclinations and attitudes of your own heart.

6. What do you need to do about them?

EPILOGUE

KNOW WHAT? YOU'LL NEVER GUESS. Even after she slammed
the door in his face he came back! He actually came to
get her. And he married her. I saw it happen!

She was ashamed—was she ever ashamed, and rightly
so I say. But he is amazing. Incredible. I can't figure it
out. He really loves her! *Loves* her, mind you. Her, the
hussy. Oh sure, she's pretty, but I mean to say. . . .

And he's such a good influence on her. Before the
wedding she cried. To do her justice, I think she'd already been trying. But when he looked at her. . . .

I don't want to sound sentimental. You know, when
she got on her knees—she actually did—get on her
knees, I mean—it was no act. Sobs. Her shoulders fairly

shook. I wouldn't ever have thought she could feel so deeply. She loves him and no wonder. He's the kind of guy that would—how can I put it?—I was going to say *bring the best out of a person* (except there wasn't all that much good to bring out). Yet now that they're together, her superficiality is gone. For the first time I can tell she's real. Of course he's not the kind of guy you could *flirt* with. Know what I think? *He makes her real.* It's a kind of miracle.

Well, so much for Mundo. She dropped him without a thought. Who can blame her? I know it sounds trite, but I think she's found her destiny, the lover she was always meant to have, the bridegroom who treats her, not like a plaything, but like a bride.

DONALD BRIDGE AND DAVID PHYPERS

More Than Tongues Can Tell

The sequel to **Spiritual Gifts and The Church**. *Foreword by David Watson.*

Pastor and Deacon of Enon Baptist Church in Sunderland, Donald Bridge and David Phypers were 'deeply hesitant about Pentecostalism'. They were cautious, faced with the first charismatic prayer group in the church. But gradually, after serious Bible study and careful prayer a new dimension of Christian living transformed their lives and the life of the fellowship.

First encounters with supernatural activities are complemented by clear reflection and thorough biblical teaching. Years of prejudice are broken down as they learn to love Catholic charismatics. Finally the renewal movement is assessed, and pointers to future growth identified.

R. T. KENDALL

Tithing

A call to serious, biblical giving.

R. T. Kendall believes that all Christians are called to tithe. What is more, if all Christians did begin to tithe, he is convinced that the church would be revitalised and the world transformed. Dr Kendall combines this bold claim with the biblical, theological and practical implications of tithing.

'It is surprising how little has been written on this subject,' he writes. 'Most Christians have heard about tithing but how many have looked at it carefully?'

Tithing is sometimes regarded as threatening, but it emerges in this book as both challenging and inspiring. Numerous exciting testimonies are told, all demonstrating in individual lives the principle which underlies *Tithing:* 'You cannot out-give the Lord'.

COLIN URQUHART

Faith For The Future

The remarkable and inspiring sequel to **WHEN THE SPIRIT COMES**

'God wants to give us all faith for the future, to believe that He will move among us in the coming years with greater power.'

After five richly-blessed years at St. Hugh's, Luton, Colin Urquhart felt that God was calling him to a new ministry – to be 'heard among the nations'. His step of faith into the unknown was the start of a miraculous adventure.

Colin's international ministry of renewal, healing and evangelism is now touching and transforming lives all over the world. Revival is brought to others because it has been experienced in the community at the Hyde, where those working with Colin have become freshly aware of the holiness and glory of God. The author of *Anything You Ask* and *In Christ Jesus* powerfully conveys in this new book that the future with God holds wonderful promise.

JAMES DOBSON

Hide Or Seek

How to build self-esteem in your child.

An epidemic of inferiority is raging throughout our society. From the moment our children enter the world they are subjected to a value system which reserves respect and esteem for only a select few. Those who fail to measure up by today's standards – particularly in the areas of intelligence and beauty – are left with feelings of inadequacy.

James Dobson exposes these pressures and the unjust value system. In their place he presents ten comprehensive strategies to cultivate self-esteem in every child.

Dr Dobson asserts that only Christian values free us from the tyranny of self and offer dignity and respect to every human being. Through this better way, children can be given the courage to *seek the best*, rather than *hide in fear and sorrow*.

DR JAMES DOBSON is a renowned child psychologist, marriage and family counsellor and author. Previous books include *Straight Talk to Men and Their Wives*.